Launching your OKR program

BASTIN GERALD

WITH SENTHIL RAJAGOPALAN

9 781794 884908

Table of
Contents

Introduction

Waiting for perfect is never as smart as making progress.

 **Seth Godin**

At this point in your OKR journey, you have probably realized two things: first, that your company can benefit greatly from this agile strategy-execution framework, and second, that you need a solid launch strategy if you want to hit the ground running with OKRs.

Launching your OKR program may be simpler than you think. If you've read the first installment in this OKR Program series, *Preparing for your OKR Program*, you know that OKRs help you bridge the "Strategy-execution gap" and achieve "stretch goals" through collaborative execution. In this book, *Launching your OKR Program*, you will learn the strategies and best practices that companies new to the OKR framework can use for successful rollouts.

Launching a solid OKR program involves writing great OKRs, choosing clear and unambiguous KPIs, aligning OKRs to ensure broader participation, and establishing accountability. Building a great check-in and review routine that establishes the execution rhythm for the whole organization increases your chances of a successful launch. Finally, knowing how to grade your OKRs and close the quarter with a well-defined process that gives adequate time for teams to reflect on their efforts, experiments and results (hits and misses) will be crucial. Sharing the lessons learned with the rest of the team and planning for the next OKR cycle completes the launch quarter.

1

How do you get started with OKRs?

You don't have to be great to start, but you have to start to be great.

 **Zig Ziglar**

Many teams that are new to the OKR framework tend to agonize over the best approach to OKRs and the "right" way to get started with this highly beneficial methodology.Business leaders know that Objectives and Key Results can give their company a competitive advantage in the market, and they want to approach their OKR launch with caution and precision in order to give their team the best chance of success.

While this might sound too simplistic to be true, it is the most effective way to begin your OKR journey and start learning and growing. Different companies will have different combinations of culture, style, processes, and values that make the DNA of their business unique. Therefore, every team or company's journey will be different; there is not one detailed approach that will be one size fits all.

There is a whole spectrum of possibilities on where and how to get started.

- At the **conservative** end of this spectrum, you'll find businesses that want to do thorough research and be comfortable with the mechanics of the framework before they put their OKRs on paper.

- At the **aggressive** end of this spectrum, you will find businesses that want to dive right in and learn along the way.

Figure 1.1: *The spectrum of adoption philosophies for businesses implementing OKRs*

Based on your unique corporate DNA, you'll find your company somewhere on this spectrum. You can prepare yourself and your team through reading exercises, knowledge-sharing sessions, conversations, meetings, and external training sessions to plan how to get started with OKRs. Whether you take the time to learn before you launch or not, what's most important is that you get started. Another more important idea to keep in mind is that adopting OKRs must be an iterative process. You may not get it right in the first quarter, but you will get a decent understanding of the framework as you begin the implementation process.

You will always learn something new every quarter. If you catalogue your team's learnings and make a point to incorporate new knowledge into the next OKR cycle, you are well on your way to a successful OKR program.

OKRs are not tasks

OKRs are not tasks that you can simply check off and mark as "done". OKRs are connected to many aspects of your company– from your strategy to your resources to your team's goals. There is an inter-connectedness to what you do in OKRs, and a certain amount of effort necessary to ensure that you're addressing the right goals.

OKRs are set, tracked, and achieved to ensure that your organization is focusing its time and

OKR Adoption: Weekly Breakdown

Task	1	2	3	4	5	...	13	...	26	→
Kickoff	▮									
Freeze Reqs & Scope		▮								
Identify Pilot Teams	▮									
Load Pilot Teams	▮									
Train Pilot Teams		▮								
Setup OKRs for Pilot Teams		▮								
Weekly Check-ins			▮▮▮▮▮▮							
First Quarter Reflect/Reset							▮			
Identify Phase 2 Teams							▮			
Load P2 Teams							▮			
Train P2 Teams							▮			
Set Up OKRs for P2 Teams							▮			
Weekly Check-ins								▮		
Quarterly Reflect/Reset									▮	

Figure 1.2: *A breakdown of what an OKR adoption might look like on a weekly basis.*

resources on the right goals. While a single employee can complete a task themself, the OKR framework is a system designed for the entire company.

Two approaches to starting your OKR program

While experts know that OKRs are not simple, many still recommend that new users just get started.

You can't expect employees to sit down and automatically know how to write OKRs on day one. It does help to include a training program to get the executive team, department leaders, and the OKR champions on the same page. This training should ideally answer any questions surrounding the use of OKRs, how to write effective OKRs, how to set up an OKR quarterly calendar, the importance of regular check-ins and weekly reviews, how to grade OKRs, and how to reflect and reset OKRs at the end of the quarter. Proper training can help get your OKR program off on the right foot. As long as you bring the executive team and department leaders on-board, large-scale rollouts across entire enterprises are possible right from the first quarter. This needs executive sponsorship, a set of OKR champions identified to provide department-level leadership, execution discipline (regular check-ins and reviews) and a conducive company culture. Companies of all sizes and in various verticals have been able to scale up rapidly with the above mentioned conditions

Some experts recommend rolling out OKRs to a small pilot team before opening up the framework to your entire business. Now, getting started doesn't necessarily mean you roll out OKRs to the 50, 100, or 1,000 people in your organization in the first month. Identify priorities and set objectives and key results with a smaller group first. Once they become more familiar with OKRs and the cadence of the framework, they can help leaders get the entire organization rolling with OKRs.

The pilot team can be:

- **A department or sub-department**: Ensure that everyone from the head of the department to your newest hire is included in the pilot team to get a sense of how top-down or bottom-up alignment will work within departments.

- **The top management team**: Include C-level executives, VPs, and other department heads in your test group in order to share top company priorities with the individuals leading the rest of the company, and to determine whether your organization should cascade goals, roll from the bottom-up, or align OKRs horizontally.

Your company's OKR program is unique to you

Remember to keep an open mind during this trial period, and be receptive to learning many new things about the way your team runs, and how your company prioritizes its goals. You will quickly learn what works and what does not work for your business. Your OKR program will be unique to your organization in three key ways:

- Structure

- Process

- Culture

Structure

Structure refers to your organization's hierarchy, as well as how you decide to practice OKRs. When beginning with this framework, you can set OKRs at the corporate and department levels. Once your team has

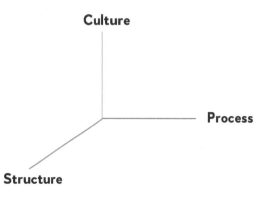

Figure 1.3: The three components that define an organization's OKR program.

gained familiarity with the framework, you can write OKRs on the team and individual levels.

In other cases, OKRs are only set at one level. If you practice OKRs at the department level, for example, the structure of departments in your company makes up the "structure" of your OKR program.

Process

Process refers to the OKR management process.

This accounts for planning sessions, weekly or biweekly check-ins, PPP meetings, mid-quarter adjustments, end-of-quarter reviews, and every conversation along the way. There are many details that you can adjust when creating your OKR process.

Culture

Your organizational culture will heavily influence your OKR program. OKRs require a learning and growth mindset within a company. Culture is uniquely shaped by the company's values, vision, as well as the senior leadership of the company. The employees' commitment to company values depends on how those at the head of the organization choose to incorporate the business's mission into their strategy and execution.

OKR is a great framework that has worked well with companies of all sizes and shapes in various industries. Using a great OKR software and taking the help of a consultant who has implemented OKRs before can help accelerate adoption. However, the best of the tools, intentions, and consulting support may not be able to make the right impact with your OKR program if the culture of your organization is not ready to adopt OKRs.

An interesting analogy for this issue may be trying to grow oranges in California vs. Nevada. You may be using the latest in agricultural technology, fertilizers and copious water, but the results will be very different in the fertile soils of California vs. the barren desert of Nevada. If you are looking at OKRs as a means to achieve stretch goals through collaborative execution, then the culture in your organization should encourage raising the bar, promote experimentation and taking risks, tolerate and learn from failures, support collaboration, celebrate innovation and require accountability.

OKR Programs & Competitive Advantage

While many people believe that strategy-execution frameworks are rigid in structure and process, OKRs are not.

If OKRs were rigid in standards and practices, then every single company could adopt them in the same way, and they would offer no competitive advantage.

OKR programs are specifically tailored to each company, providing a competitive advantage for a business in their specific field and market.

Since you must find your own unique OKR DNA, the framework requires a few quarters of iteration, trial, and error in order to hit your stride. If you understand this conceptually, you will be able to progress steadily towards your ideal OKR position.

Top Four Reasons Companies Postpone OKRs

The prospect of learning, implementing, and perfecting a new framework can seem daunting to many companies. Because of this, business leaders tend to find reasons to put off implementation. Below are the four most common reasons that companies elect to postpone their OKR programs– and why you shouldn't use each excuse.

1. We don't have enough time for OKRs

Shark Tank Judge and Entrepreneur, Mark Cuban, says he worries about the **Return on his**

time (ROT) when he looks for investments, not just ROI. Anyone in business can tell you that time is a precious– and scarce– resource. However, *"I don't have time"* is the worst possible excuse for not going ahead with OKRs.

To help understand why this isn't a good excuse, consider yoga. You don't put off going to classes because you're not flexible enough– you go to classes in order to become flexible. So if the reason you can't commit to rolling out OKRs is because you "don't have the time," that is all the more reason to implement OKRs. OKRs help you manage your time and resources effectively and efficiently– they do not add to your ever-growing to-do list.

2. Our leaders need to be trained on the standard process

As discussed earlier, the biggest misconception with OKR rollouts is that there is a standardized template for OKRs that you must learn, master, and apply to your business. This simply isn't true.

It's not a bad thing to want to read up on the OKR framework and understand the general "rules" of the process. However, it doesn't take multiple quarters to learn this information. Setting aside an hour or a couple of hours per week for a month to learn the basics is more than enough to prepare you to launch your OKR program.

3. We need to find a good consultant to guide us

If you can find a seasoned OKR consultant to coach you before you get going with OKRs, that is excellent. A great OKR consultant will teach you the general structure and process aspects of OKRs, and help you create your own unique OKR program that integrates seamlessly into your company's culture.

But consultants do not usually sign on for long-term commitments. Often, you will not have the time or capital to have a three- to six-month implementation cycle. Many consultants offer five-hour DIY courses and certifications. So, while there is nothing wrong with getting someone to guide you, finding a consultant is not a prerequisite.

4. We need to find the perfect software tool

Another misconception is that you have to get an OKR software tool before you can get started with the OKR framework. While software can help manage and scale OKR programs within a company, it's most certainly not a prerequisite.

Pilot teams can usually stay aligned for one or two quarters by using spreadsheets or PowerPoint presentations. During this time, your implementation manager can hunt for the right software while your other leaders are gaining familiarity and skill with the OKR process.

By the time your leaders are ready to roll out OKRs to the rest of the company, you will be ready with a software tool that works for your company.

Once again: getting started is important. Don't keep making excuses and put off your OKR program; define the scope of your pilot team, and start learning.

OKR Quick Start Guide

Here is a quick to-do list to help you get started with the first quarter of your OKR program:

- Select a pilot team

- Define 3-5 OKRs for the pilot team members

- Keep alignments between OKRs simple

- Incorporate OKR check-ins into your weekly schedule

- Remove roadblocks to achieving the key results you set out to accomplish regularly

- Communicate change in priorities and plans effectively and immediately

- Document learnings regularly, on a weekly, biweekly, or monthly basis

- Reflect and reset at the end of the quarter

This list may seem deceptively simple, but getting started is simple. It is intended to be. Each step of this guide is covered in more detail later in this book.

This simple list is just a primer to help you get started. Once the ball is rolling, you can hire expert consultants and implement sophisticated software to help you master this process—just be careful not to make them prerequisites to getting started.

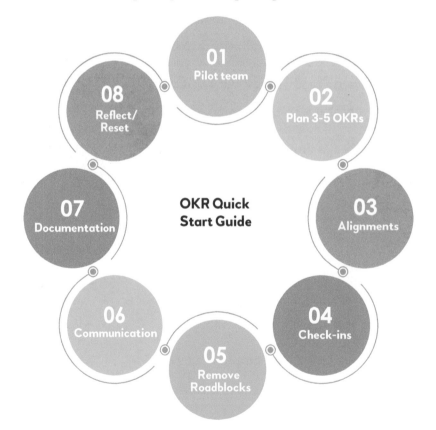

2

How do you choose your OKR levels?

What are OKR levels?

Let's review how leaders can go about setting up and rolling out OKRs at their company.

Every company, typically, has overarching goals that they want to see fulfilled based on their long-term strategy or company values. On a smaller scale, all companies have multiple departments that are responsible for specific objectives and projects. In some cases, there are cross-functional teams that work together to solve a problem. Then, finally, we have individual employees working in all these departments, and they are responsible for their own projects or tasks.

These are the four levels at which you can set OKRs, also commonly referred to as **OKR Levels**:

- Company Level OKRs

- Department Level OKRs

- Cross-functional Team OKRs

- Individual OKRs

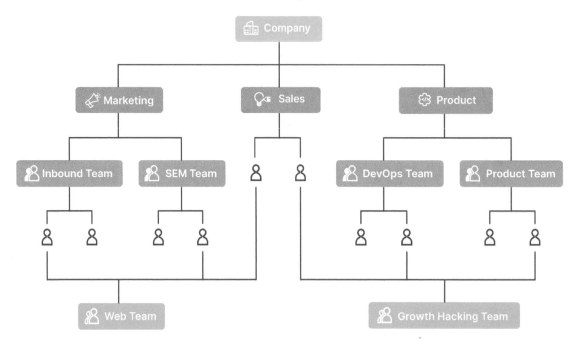

Figure 2.1: Company hierarchy showing what teams, departments, and levels could have their own set of OKRs.

Company level OKRs

First, leaders typically start at the company level and set up corporate OKRs (or company OKRs). Corporate OKRs are usually set on an annual basis. Once you settle on three or four impactful objectives for the company for the year, you should track their progress using 3 to 5 key results each.

At the company level, for example, you might have an OKR to grow the business. An example Objective could be to **"Grow revenue."**

Achieving your Objective

Let's say a quarter or a year has gone by after setting your company objective to "Grow Revenue". How do you know if you have grown and hit those revenue targets? In order to help measure progress throughout the life of your objective, you must set key results that will help you answer this question. For our objective to grow revenue, one of the key results can be:

- Establish Europe as a notable region by generating $3M in new ARR

A second key result may be about increasing expansion revenue. You can choose to drive expansion with clients with high potential for using and benefitting from your product.

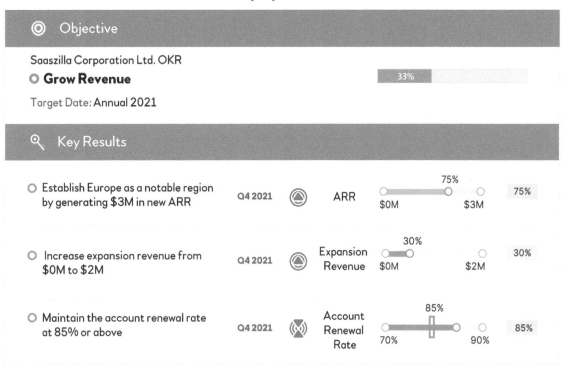

Company Level OKRs

A third key result may be about retaining customers and accounts. In this case, the key result can be: "Maintain the account renewal rate at 85% or above."

All of these key results are measurable and address key outcomes in your organization that can be used to determine the success of your objective to Grow Revenue. If these three key results are complete, the revenue of the company will necessarily grow.

Department level OKRs

Achieving a corporate OKR such as growing revenue is a company-wide and multi-department pursuit.

In order to succeed in increasing revenue, multiple departments must be mobilized. For example, the marketing department has to generate new leads and uncover new revenue opportunities. They also might need to identify and target new markets to grow the business.

The sales team then has to nurture the leads provided by marketing and then execute the sales process to help bring on new clients.

Figure 2.2: Each of these departments is necessary in order to complete the company-level objective.

The research & development team will have to work on new products and improve existing products to keep up with market and customer demands.

Finally, the product, manufacturing, or services teams might need to create additional production capacity, introduce new manufacturing lines, or open manufacturing plants to support all these growth goals.

All new projects or to-do-lists are derived from our original corporate OKR to grow revenue, which informs departmental OKRs in each area of the company.

Let us expand on what each of these departments will have to do to achieve their targets and help make the company OKR a reality.

Let's start with the sales team. One of the corporate-level key results was to establish Europe as a notable region by generating $3M in New ARR. The sales team can say that one of its objectives is to "Penetrate the Italian market."

A few key results can be used to measure this objective. One of the key results might be to open a new sales office in Milan, Italy. The key result will be: "Establish a new sales office in Milan." If you complete this key result in Q1, it will give you about three more quarters (Q2, Q3, Q4) to ramp up and ensure a solid execution in the Italian market.

The second key result could be: "Onboard a VP of Sales for Italy." It might need to be done

Department OKRs

◎ Objective		
Sales Department OKRs		
⊙ Penetrate the Italian Market		42%
Target Date: Annual 2021		

⚷ Key Results						
○ Establish a new sales office in Milan	Q4 2021	⚑	Open Sales Office	50% ○——○ 60% 90% ○	50%
○ Onboard a VP of Sales for Italy	Q4 2021	⊘%	Percentage Tracked	35% ○—○ 0% 100% ○	35%
○ Generate 50 leads per week in the region	Q4 2021	◉	Leads	15 ○—○ 0 50 ○	15%
○ Acquire 40 new logos in the region to increase our footprint	Q4 2021	◉	Logos	10 ○—○ 0 40 ○	10%

earlier than the end of Q1, and thus can be set as the Q1 Key Result.

Once you have the location set up and the VP of sales is hired, you can then have a couple of key results to test the market. The third key result for that quarter can be: "Generate at least 50 leads per week in the region." And finally, the fourth key result can be: "Acquire 40 new logos in the region to increase our footprint." With all these key results set up, you can focus and execute aggressively for the next three quarters. You will have a local office in Milan, hire a regional VP of Sales, and have demonstrated the ability to generate leads and onboard logos.

This Sales OKR ties back to the corporate-level key result to increase the number of countries in operation from 10 to 15. In many companies, setting corporate and department-level OKRs is more than enough to get rolling with your OKR program and start to see significant results from quarter to quarter. Horizontal alignment between departments will help each sector of the company fulfill their target outcomes— for example, the sales team might ask for support from HR, marketing, and customer success to help meet their key results.

Cross-functional team level OKRs

In most company's OKR programs, departments are not in silos that can operate without the support of other teams. In fact, you'll find that many key results won't be successful if they are owned and executed by one department. Instead, you'll need individuals from various departments to help fulfill a specific key result.

Let us review the OKR to "Penetrate the Italian Market." Opening a sales office in Milan could be the responsibility of the company's Facilities Management department, while the Sales department leads the initiative because they are responsible for ensuring the office is successful.

The process of finding and onboarding a VP of Sales will be influenced by what the Sales department wants in their next leader, but ultimately the interview and onboarding process must be supported by the HR department and the Chief Executive's Office.

For initiatives that require the full attention of players in multiple departments, leaders should consider creating a cross-functional team of the right employees to own and execute the OKR. Whether a business elects to have separate departments that are horizontally aligned or cross-functional team OKRs, the communication and clarity of OKRs must be prioritized above all else.

For example, the OKR "Improve conversion rates across all stages of the sales funnel" may require support from the Customer Support, Marketing, and even Content teams. Potential customers need support and attention in order to convert from leads to signed clients. While the Sales team might take charge of an OKR like this, individuals from other departments

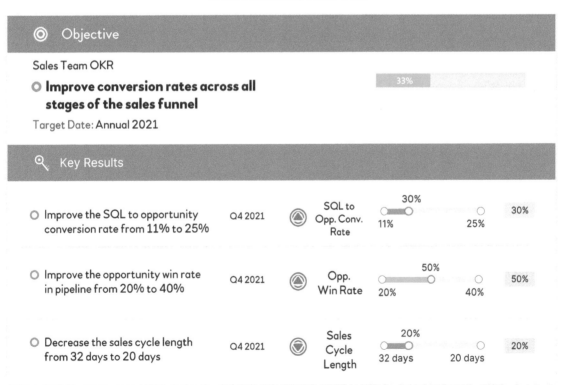

Cross-Functional Team OKR

will be included on this OKR in order to properly distribute the responsibility for meeting the targets outlined in the key results.

Individual OKRs

Finally, companies can choose to set OKRs at the individual level. Employees can have their own OKRs that they are accountable for. These OKRs are commonly informed by department- or team-level key results.

For example, the department-level key result "Generate at least 50 leads per week in the region" could potentially become the objective for the Demand Generation Director or Marketing Director.

If the director needs 50 new leads per week from the Italian market, they will ask themselves what steps they need to take or outcomes they need to see in order to help generate these leads.

The director's solution might be to run Google Ads, LinkedIn Ads, or run advertisements in newspapers or magazines.

Additionally, they can elect to write some PR announcements that the company is entering the Italian market, as well as arrange a press conference to get the message out. All these initiatives create awareness in the market.

Once awareness increases, potential clients are more likely to find the business. A website or landing page can help promote sign-ups and demos, generating new leads.

What is the ideal way to roll out OKRs?

Like anything with the OKR framework, the "ideal" way to roll out OKRs entirely depends on your organization. It's important to consider your company's experience with OKRs and the maturity of your OKR program. These will be significant factors in deciding which levels you want to set OKRs at.

If your business is just starting out with OKRs, then having too many OKR levels in play will result in a complex and potentially confusing OKR environment.

When it comes to companies that are just starting off with OKRs, it's a lot smarter to limit yourself to two levels and add more when needed than it is to start off with granular levels and not end up needing them. The general recommendation for companies just getting started with OKRs is rolling out company and department-level OKRs first, and running your program for a few quarters before adding any cross-functional team or individual-level OKRs.

With this approach, all team members will understand:

- The function of OKRs

- How to create objectives

- How to write a good Key Result

- How to measure key result progress

If you first introduce employees to OKRs at the individual level, employees may fear that they are being evaluated and micromanaged. This concern can limit their willingness to set aspirational and stretch objectives. Meanwhile, if you start with company-wide and department OKRs and then slowly expand your OKR program as needed, employees will have a better understanding of the core principles of OKRs and how they can stretch their personal goals and contribute to the higher-level goals of the company.

Rolling out your OKRs

One of the most important decisions to make when launching your OKR program is to decide which levels you will set OKRs at. Be sure that you are considering your company's history, the kind of goals you want to achieve, and your team's familiarity with OKRs.

	Corporate OKRs	Department OKRs	Team OKRs	Individual OKRs
Get a feel for OKRs	✓	✗	✗	✗
Department Centric	✓	✓	✗	✗
Individual Centric	✓	✗	✗	✓
Department Centric & Individuals as needed	✓	✓	✗	✓
Cross Functional Initiatives	✗	✗	✓	✗

Figure 2.3: *This table shows the different methods for introducing OKRs to your company. By enabling these OKR levels, you can approach OKRs in a way that works best for your organization.*

Most businesses use two or three levels over the course of their OKR program. You don't have to pick one level or approach and stick with it. The beauty of the OKR framework is that it is an agile way to execute your strategy quarter to quarter as your company grows and your needs change.

3

How do you write good OKRs?

In recent years, strategy-execution frameworks have become more important in businesses. For many teams, there's a gap between the strategy they plan in a given quarter or year, and their execution. This is a gap that strategy-execution frameworks aim to close. Especially in the past year, as teams across the globe moved to remote or hybrid-model work, it has become vital for companies to have a framework to organize their strategy into actionable steps.

OKRs are one such framework that has gained attention and credibility in mainstream business. Industry-leaders such as Google, Netflix, Spotify, and Amazon use OKRs to accomplish more with precision and purpose.

The structure of OKRs is as follows: a qualitative and aspirational objective statement, followed by three to five quantitative outcomes that help determine the success of the objective statement.

The OKR structure is an easy thing for everyone to understand, but the forethought and planning that must go into the process of writing a great OKR isn't always as straightforward as we would like it to be. In this article, we'll break down the process for writing a strong OKR.

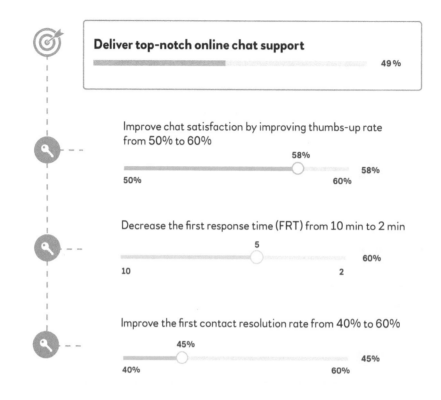

Figure 3.1: This is a well-formulated OKR with a clear, memorable objective and three measurable, relevant key results.

How do you write good Objectives?

The first part of a strong OKR is the objective.

An objective is a statement that articulates what you want to accomplish. Ideally, this statement is ambitious, brief, and memorable. The set objective statements should make the top priority of the company, department, team, or individual clear for a given quarter. Team members should ideally be able to read this at the beginning of the quarter and remember it without referring back to their OKR software or manager.

When writing an objective, ask yourself the following questions:

- Is the objective inspiring?

- Is the objective simple and specific?

- Is there alignment with other objectives?

- Is the objective time-bound?

- Does the objective stretch the team?

1. Is the Objective Inspiring?

Companies often make the mistake of choosing Objectives that are just marginal improvements to their existing KPIs.

As we know, KPIs are measurable metrics typically used to monitor a company's or a team's progress. Even though they differ from industry to industry, they are widely understood and used by most companies.

OKRs, on the other hand, are ambitious statements (Objectives) broken down into specific, actionable outcomes (Key Results).

If your Objectives are just to improve your existing KPIs, then they will not be effective. For example:

- Improve Operational Cash flow by 10% this quarter.

- Improve Average-Order-Value by 20%.

Your teams are already working on these KPI improvements. Hence, if you set attainable and relatively easy Objectives, that might not help your company make considerable leaps in growth and innovation.

Your objectives must be inspirational. Large and successful companies choose inspirational and ambitious OKRs for their teams. Ambitious objectives encourage companies to push themselves to reach targets they previously thought were unattainable. Also, reaching those objectives means that the company has experienced considerable, tangible growth that meaningfully contributes to the business, their customers, or society as a whole.

When setting ambitious quality objectives, you must find a balance between stretch goals and unattainable goals. If an objective is unreasonable, your team might get discouraged and potentially lose interest in that objective. It could also lead to employee burnout and can drastically affect morale.

To strike the right balance, choose objectives with at least a 70% chance of attainment for that quarter.

2. Is the Objective Simple and Specific?

Your objective must be specific and straightforward. Your employees and other stakeholders should easily and quickly understand what you are trying to achieve.

Specific objectives encourage your team to come up with the right strategy and action items to help achieve them. It also helps them choose the right key results and the right departments to accomplish them.

Here are a few examples of clear-cut and simple objectives:

- Customer Success: "Deliver top-notch online chat support"

- Client Success: "Launch a coaching program for clients"

- Sales: "Strengthen Pre-Sales Process"

- Marketing: "Establish Active Resellers Channel"

- SEO: "Improve Domain Authority"

As you can see from these above examples, the objectives focus on a specific problem or outcome. All team members within a department can quickly grasp what they need to focus on and help develop the right key results. Anyone outside the department or company also can easily understand what that team is focusing on.

3. Is there Alignment with other Objectives?

Setting up OKRs should never be a one-person mission. Also, it is not solely up to the leadership to set up the objectives and then cascade them down to the team. This is another common challenge many companies face when they first set OKRs. The leader is enthused about a specific goal, sets it up as an objective, and then forwards it to the department heads to enforce. Unfortunately, this approach causes unwanted tension and can also risk the objective being ignored as the weeks go by.

Alignment is hence a critical element of setting up successful objectives.

| Focus | Alignment | Commitment | Tracking | Stretching |

Figure 3.2: *The five key benefits or elements of OKRs. Here, alignment is highlighted.*

Here's an illustration. Let's say the Marketing Department sets an Objective "Create a Robust Lead Generation System". The Marketing Department is usually made up of individual teams or sub-departments such as:

- Paid Search team

- Social media team

- Content Marketing team

- PR team, etc.

Each of these teams and their team members are responsible for helping the Marketing Department set up a lead generation system.

Each department might have a specific objective that ties into the department's objective:

- Social Media Team Objective: "Grow social media presence"

- Email Marketing Team Objective: "Create email campaigns to generate leads"

- Content Team Objective: "Create Bottom-of-the-Funnel Content to drive lead acquisition"

Each of these Team Objectives then has corresponding Key Results. When all team objectives are complete, the department objective will also be complete.

There must be alignment between departments, teams, and individual contributors. You should continually brainstorm with team members before you finalize your objective.

4. Is the Objective Time-Bound?

According to tech entrepreneur and *Shark Tank* investor Robert Herjavec, "Any goal without a deadline is just a dream".

As mentioned earlier, there is nothing wrong with setting up an audacious vision. Big goals have a motivating effect on employees. Most of your team members want to be challenged;

they want to participate in a collective vision that motivates them to get out of bed each day and come to work.

However, if your goals or objectives do not have a set timeline, it will cause a significant breakdown in the process. Without a clear timeline for that objective, it affects the planning and the necessary action you must take.

Therefore, most OKRs are set on a quarterly or annual basis, though some companies might have one or two multi-year OKRs. Regardless of the timeline, having a precise end date helps your team formulate the right plan and set up the exact key results required.

Let's look at some of the Department OKR examples from before:

- Sales: "Strengthen Pre-Sales Process"

- Marketing: "Establish Active Resellers Channel"

- SEO: "Improve Domain Authority"

To increase the odds of attaining these objectives, ensure that you have chosen the right timeline, and then set up the Key Results to aid these Objectives.

There is a chance you might not reach your Objective for a quarter or period– that's okay. Even if you reach 70% of your Objective, you would have made tremendous progress.

5. Does the Objective Stretch the Team?

Have you heard the expression "under-promise and over-deliver"? There's a term in management to indicate when this happens a lot– it's called "sandbagging". Sandbagging is when teams set up easily attainable goals that they know they will reach or exceed.

It looks good from the outside when you notice a team or company always attaining its goals.

However, there are both short-term and long-term consequences for sandbagging.

Sandbagging creates an environment that is not at all challenging, which naturally decreases overall engagement. It will also hurt the company's competitiveness in the marketplace when everyone else races to develop and market superior products.

One of the key elements of OKRs is the concept of "Stretching".

Focus   Alignment   Commitment   Tracking   Stretching

Figure 3.3: *The five key benefits or elements of OKRs. Here, stretching is highlighted.*

You must set goals and objectives that are aspirational, and even slightly beyond reach. It will allow your team to grow and not be complacent. It also helps your employees and your entire company expand their comfort zone and push themselves to work harder and smarter.

Ask yourself and your team all of the above questions when writing objectives for the quarter, and ensure the answer to each question is "yes" before finalizing your objectives. In order to get the most out of the OKR framework, it's important that you meet these criteria.

Remember that objectives should not be measurable in and of themselves. Objectives are meant to speak towards your strategy, and break down a company's top priorities into goals that can be focused on within a quarter. Key results will help you measure the success of this objective, so there is no need to add KPIs in the Objective itself. Instead, ensure that your objective addresses the most important thing you have to focus on in the quarter.

A poorly-written objective will be vague and uninspired. For example, "Refresh our onboarding process." This is technically a goal, but it's unambitious. You can rewrite this goal with the proper energy and inspiration behind it, changing it to: "Deliver a world-class onboarding experience for new hires."

How do you write good Key Results?

Writing good key results is, at times, a little more complicated than writing good Objectives. Key results must provide quantitative outcomes that help you measure the success of your objective. In order to measure what matters most for your goal, key results must be mutually exclusive and collectively exhaustive. The last thing any team wants is empty targets that are achievable, but don't actually make an impact on the objective itself.

To create strong, qualitative key results for your objectives, ask yourself the following questions:

- Are the key results aligned?

- Are the key results measurable?

- Are the key results the same as your team's day-to-day tasks?

- Are any key results paired?

- Are the key results controllable?

- Is there an accountability system for key results?

1. Are the Key Results Aligned?

When choosing quality objectives, it's important to always stay aligned and in sync with the company and departmental priorities. This applies when selecting key results as well. If your key results are not aligned with the objectives, then it will confuse your team members. It will also lower your chances of achieving your objectives.

For example, let's use a Marketing Department objective to "Create a Robust Lead Generation Engine".

From here, the VP of Marketing should discuss setting up the right key results with each Marketing team lead. In turn, each team leader should create respective Objectives and Key Results to contribute and align to the Department's Objective.

- Department Objective: Create a Robust Lead Generation Engine

- Department KR1: Generate 100 leads from all the organic social media channels

- Department KR2: Launch three new email campaigns

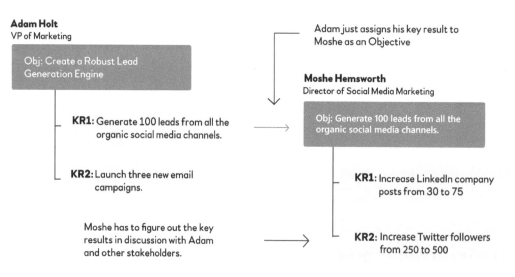

Cascading an OKR from the Top-Down
Assign a KR as Objective

Figure 3.4: An example of how an OKR is cascaded downward from a department to a team.

One of these key results can also be an objective for one of the teams. For example, the social media team might choose "Generate 100 leads from all organic social media channels" as one of their objectives. Then they would create key results for this objective.

Objective: Generate 100 leads from all the organic social media channels

   KR1: Increase LinkedIn company posts from 30 to 75

   KR 2: Increase Twitter followers from 250 to 500

These key results are then assigned to the members of the social media team.

2. Are the Key Results Measurable?

As discussed earlier, key results must be numeric and measurable. They should specify a set goal that you must accomplish to progress the objective. A common mistake made in OKR implementation is picking unspecific key results that can't be easily measured.

Let's say one of your objectives is "Grow new revenue". It's a clear and straightforward goal. Let's say you choose vague key results such as:

- KR 1: Increase sales calls.

- KR 2: Change pricing model.

- KR 3: Increase renewals.

Even though the key results are the right action steps, they don't provide clarity for your team. With these key results, your team would not be sure how many calls they need to make, or what changes to make to the pricing model.

Instead, your key results must be specific and concise, such as:

Objective: Grow new revenue

KR 1: Increase the outbound sales calls per SDR from 50/day to 70/day

KR 2: Increase the % of annual subscriptions out of total subscriptions sold from 60% to 85%

KR 3: Increase the trial-to-paid plan conversion rate from 15% to 25%

These examples of key results can help Sales Managers and the Sales & Renewal teams to focus on the right activities to help reach them.

3. Are the Key Results the same as your team's day-to-day tasks?

Occasionally, key results are confused with daily tasks. As the name suggests, "key results" are specific results that you need to achieve, while "tasks" are day-to-day responsibilities that your team must complete.

Let's take the social media team in the Marketing Department as an example. The following are some of their daily or weekly tasks:

- Create and update content schedules

- Create images for social media sharing

- Get training on the updated version of Hootsuite

- Analyze metrics on a weekly basis

The above tasks highlight what the team needs to do to ensure that they stay on top of their projects. The completion of these tasks might even be tied to their performance reviews. Key results have to be numeric and have to stretch your team beyond their daily and normal capabilities. Here are examples of good key results for a social media team to improve online reach:

Objective: Make social media channels a hub for engaging with followers

KR 1: Increase CTR in social media posts from 2% to 4%

KR 2: Onboard 5 LinkedIn influencers as brand evangelists

KR 3: Enhance profile to increase profile visits from 40k to 60k every month.

4. Are any Key Results Paired?

We've consistently mentioned that Key Results need to be quantifiable to be effective. However, a common mistake made by teams implementing OKRs is that they set too many quantifiable key results. In their haste to achieve more in that period, teams make the mistake of ignoring the quality of the key results.

Pairing both quantity-focused and quality-focused key results is crucial. Otherwise, you'll end up hitting all your metrics at the expense of quality and customer satisfaction.

Let's take an example of an OKR set by a company related to increasing lead flow.

Objective: Increase lead flow

KR 1: Acquire 5 new referrals from existing customers

KR2: Onboard 5 new MDRs (Marketing Development Representatives)

KR2: Improve the MQL to SQL conversion ratio from 40% to 70%

At the outset, this OKR seems like it meets the characteristics of a strong, quality OKR. However, the KRs in this example are all focused on converting and onboarding existing leads, and growing the team.

If you are converting existing leads, but not working to generate more leads, you could have a situation where your ability to generate leads does not actually improve, putting a ceiling on the growth you can have in this area.

With that in mind, here's a revised OKR:

Objective: Increase lead flow

KR 1: Acquire 5 new referrals from existing customers

KR 2: Onboard 5 new MDRs (Marketing Development Representatives)

KR 3: Improve the MQL to SQL conversion ratio from 40% to 70%

KR 4: Generate 150 demo sign-ups from blog

KR 5: Launch email marketing campaign

KR4 and KR5 ensure that you are taking strides to generate new leads. Once you properly pair these key results, you can be confident that you are approaching your objective in a holistic way.

The same principle applies to other areas of business, such as:

- Customer Service: It's great to add new features, but you must also ensure that there are fewer bugs overall.

- Website: You can aim for higher website traffic, but if your bounce rate is high, then you are not converting enough website visitors.

- Content Marketing: It's not a bad idea to publish more content, but if your content is not high-quality and converting readers to leads, then your content marketing program is not profitable.

5. Are the Key Results Controllable?

Another quality criterion to keep in mind when choosing key results is that they must be controllable. In other words, you should have the ability to influence the outcome of the key results.

Set key results that your team members can act on and measure. If you choose key results that you cannot influence or those that depend on external factors, they will not align with the objective.

For example, let's say one of your Marketing Team Objectives is to "Improve website traffic significantly through organic channel". You should refrain from using KRs that rely on external factors, such as:

- KR 1: Avoid being flagged by Google algorithms

- KR 2: Have other sites automatically link to us

Both these examples denote things that you cannot control. Your KRs must target things that you can influence internally. Here are some examples of good Key Results for the same Objective:

Objective: Improve website traffic significantly through organic channel

KR1: Optimize website performance by reducing avg page loading time from 4 sec to 2 sec

KR2: Get at least 100 high-quality backlinks per month

KR3: Identify 25 primary keywords and publish blog posts for each keyword

You can assign the above key results to your teams and team members. They can then easily track and measure the performance of these KRs and report on their progress.

6. Is There an Accountability System for Key Results?

Focus   Alignment   Commitment   Tracking   Stretching

Figure 3.5: The key benefits and elements of OKRs. Here, tracking is highlighted.

Another essential element of success with the OKR methodology is "Tracking". If you are not adequately tracking and measuring your progress, then you will not know whether you are moving in the right direction.

Measurements are not new for companies. Whether you are a startup or a large organization, you already have some system in place to report on your KPIs:

- Sales: CRM

- Marketing: Marketing automation platforms, analytics tools

- Customer Service: Ticketing systems

- Engineering Teams: Software bug tracking system

- Finance: Profit-and-loss statements, balance sheet

As Peter Drucker famously said, "What gets measured, gets managed". We also believe that what gets measured gets tracked and therefore gets improved.

Most of the example key results we have discussed so far are easily trackable in your CRM, marketing platforms, or project management tools. However, the additional element of periodic check-ins (usually on a weekly basis) allows everyone to know where they stand and how far the team is in their quest to reach the objective.

We recommend weekly check-ins to ensure that everyone is on the same page. You can do this by updating everyone at your regular team meetings or even Company Town Halls (for Corporate Objectives). You can also use an OKR software or tool to provide visibility to all stakeholders.Periodic check-ins and accountability also help you make the necessary course corrections if you are far off from your goal or heading in the wrong direction.

By ensuring that your key results are high-quality, you set yourself and your team up for success in the coming quarter and can measure the progress of your objective with clarity and focus. Creating quality OKRs is the first step in achieving your ambitious goals and starting off a new quarter strong with focus, alignment, and clarity.

How can you write quality key results using the SMART goals approach?

Anyone looking to learn more about properly setting and managing goals has probably read about SMART goals. Here's a refresher: SMART is an acronym to help you set plausible goals for you and your team. This stands for: Specific, Measurable, Attainable, Realistic, and Time-bound.

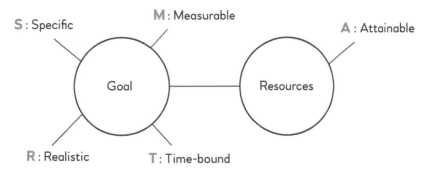

SMART GOAL

Figure 3.6: What each element of a SMART goal refers to in a key result.

The more you read about key results and SMART goals, you may start to recognize the similarities between the two.

Let's take a closer look at each requirement of a SMART goal:

S: Specific

Making your goal specific means that there should be no ambiguity about the topic or extent of your goal. Anyone reading it should be able to understand your goal, precisely. For example, if you have a goal to grow annual recurring revenue (ARR), you should not simply write your goal as: "Grow ARR". Instead, you should provide a specific number. For example, "Grow ARR to $4M".

M: Measurable

Ensuring that your goal is measurable is an important part of staying on track from week to week. You will not be able to determine when you have achieved your goal if you cannot measure it. So, when setting a goal, you should specify what you are measuring– such as the number of leads or number of conversions. You can track your progress towards your goal on a weekly basis.

A: Attainable

When you set goals, they should always be attainable with what your team, department, or organization has on hand. This attribute speaks towards the capacity of your employees and capability of resources that you have available in your organization at this point. If you have a goal that is specific and measurable, but you don't have any employees available to work on it, or don't have the budget to execute it, then the goal isn't useful, and it won't succeed.

R: Realistic

While the attributes "attainable" and "realistic" may sound like synonyms, they address unique characteristics of a goal. While the achievability of a goal refers to how attainable it is with the resources of the organization, the attribute "realistic" refers to the target itself. Has the department or team assigned to this goal completed something like this in the past? Will they have a tried and true method to achieve this target? Or are they starting from scratch? Is there a precedent that can tell your team this target is realistic for them?

T: Time-bound

Finally, you need to ensure that your goal has a distinct deadline that adds urgency and importance to the target. While you might have a goal to revamp your marketing materials, very little will be accomplished if you do not have a deadline to prompt yourself and others to get moving on what needs to be done.

Goals should meet all of the requirements outlined by the SMART acronym. These characteristics build on one another to create a solid goal that is informative, unambiguous, time-bound, and measurable. If you meet all of these attributes, you'll have a solid, well-structured goal.

Many OKR champions report struggling with learning to write solid, well-structured key results in the early stages of their OKR program; SMART goals can actually help with this.

Let's take a look at a high-quality key result:

"Increase the number of students enrolled in primary class from 0 to 24 in Q3."

Already, you can probably tell that this key result has met many of the requirements of a SMART goal. First, this key result is specific and unambiguous. Second, it is measurable, with

Figure 3.7: *How each element of a SMART goal is included in a well-structured key result.*

a clear metric— the number of students— that you can track over a period of time. Third, it is attainable, meaning that this key result can be assigned to an individual who will be responsible for enrolling students.

Fourth, is this key result realistic? We would need some background information on the owner of the key result. However, if there's a precedent, and a similar goal has been set and achieved before, the answer is yes.

Finally, this key result specifies it should be completed within quarter three— a reasonable timeframe for a key result that's set at the beginning of the quarter.

This key result meets all the requirements of SMART goals. In fact, all great key results will qualify as SMART goals; however, not all the SMART goals you write will make good key results.

Key results have another requirement that other SMART goals don't: they must be informed by the high-level goals of the organization or department and account for any alignments or dependencies. While individual entrepreneurs might use SMART goals to keep their personal or professional development on track, organizations need to use a goal-setting process that is attentive to the strategy, resources, and trajectory of the company as a whole.

To account for these things, it's wise to set key results based on lagging or leading KPIs, so your team is measuring what matters most for your business success. Key results can also be activity-based or even address non-measurable targets such as hiring a new department head, or creating a new onboarding system. Regardless of the metrics used in your key results, you still must address the five attributes of a SMART goal. From there, you can align targets and track targets knowing that you have a well-written and well-structured goal.

How do you ensure you have the right mix of Key Results?

While writing objectives is relatively straightforward, many teams struggle with the art of creating a good key result. There is some confusion surrounding what separates a good key result from a bad key result.

To help demystify the process of writing a great key result, consider these four classes of key results:

- Lagging indicator key results

- Leading indicator key results

- Activity-based key results

- Paired/Balancing key results

For each OKR level, not all of these classes need to be used, but generally speaking, your key results will be a combination of these four classes.

Lagging Indicator KRs

The first key question when writing key results is: how will you achieve your objective?

The best way to measure objective progress is to have KPI-based key results. KPIs, or key performance indicators, give concrete measurements of key outcomes in your business. If business execution is a road trip, OKRs are the destination you're driving to, and KPIs are the information on your car's dashboard– like your speed, fuel level, and engine temperature– that indicates how your car is doing along the way.

KPIs become key results when they are measured, set as a target, and given a deadline.

Your key results for an objective must be mutually exclusive and collectively exhaustive. So, if your key results are all 100% complete, your objective must necessarily be complete.

Usually, you will have some KPIs already identified at the company level. As you go down through the organization to a more operational level, it may be more difficult to find the right KPIs. In most cases, though, you will be able to find a KPI that will help indicate if you have achieved your objective or not.

In other strategy-execution methodologies, such as Wildly Important Goals (The WIG Methodology) there is the concept of a lagging indicator. Lagging indicators are the metrics that measure the success of the objective directly. These can be difficult to measure, and are usually only measured towards the top layer of an organization.

Topical key results are highly effective at helping you determine if you have achieved your objective. With lagging indicators, you usually have a baseline KPI available that you have recorded for multiple quarters.

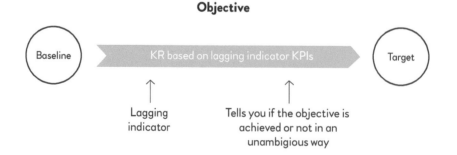

Figure 3.8: A representation of lagging indicators.

Lagging indicators help measure production and performance accurately. These KPIs indicate if you have achieved your objective in clear, unambiguous terms. While these are the KPIs that provide the most clarity, they can be difficult to monitor directly, and there may be a limited number of these available to be tracked in a company.

An example of a lagging indicator is the number of sales closed within a week. This number is not something that your organization can directly affect— instead, you need to do other activities or tasks that will impact this number. However, the number of sales closed is a great indicator of your revenue and the effectiveness of your marketing and sales teams.

Creating key results from these indicators should be your first step when writing a new OKR.

Leading Indicator KRs

Meanwhile, leading indicators help show leaders how to produce desired results.

For example, in Sales, you might want to hit a certain amount of revenue. In order to achieve that amount, you calculate that you will need to get 5,000 leads per week.

The amount of revenue is a lagging indicator. This is the outcome you want to produce. The number of leads is a leading indicator— or how you go about reaching the outcome you want.

Figure 3.9: A representation of leading indicators.

The sales process from "number of leads" to "revenue" has many steps in between. A salesperson needs to complete demos with clients, write a proposal, and negotiate a deal in order to reach the closed sale and revenue. So, the number of leads is a leading indicator, as it comes before the closed sale/revenue marker in the sales process. If you measure leading indicators closer to this endpoint, such as the number of proposals written, or number of deals negotiated, you will have a stronger KPI that has a more direct impact on the lagging indicator you're trying to measure.

At lower levels of the company, you might not have as many lagging indicators to track for department- or team-level OKRs. However, you will probably be able to define leading indicators.

So, if the Sales department has an assigned objective to "Substantially Grow Revenue," they will not use "Revenue" as a KPI. Instead, they will use leading indicators that will necessarily affect revenue— such as the customer renewal rate, lead to sales conversions, and customer churn.

Key results based on leading indicators should be used when lagging indicators do not make sense for the given objective, or if OKRs are set at lower, more operational levels of the company.

Activity-Based Key Results

Then, you have activity-based key results. Activities are the tangible tasks and targets that employees produce with their day-to-day work. Companies should avoid using activities as their first means of setting key results. However, at the team and individual levels, it makes more sense to set activity-based key results.

The more granular OKRs become, the more likely you will see activity-based key results.

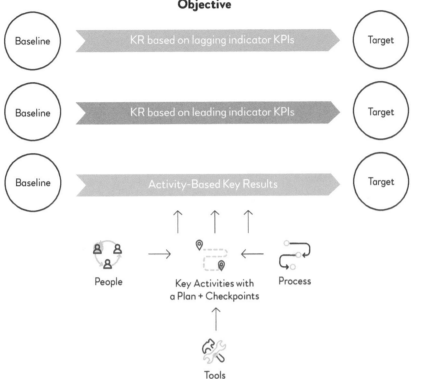

Figure 3.10: *A representation of activity-based key results.*

When you delegate key results to a department, team, or individual, key results like these are ultimately necessary to help achieve the overall objective.

These key results might not necessarily be attached to a KPI. It is not uncommon to have milestone-tracked activity-based key results. In general, this class of key result will be handled and achieved using people, processes, and tools.

Balancing Key Results or Paired Key Results

Once you are done creating key results using lagging indicators, leading indicators, as well as activity-based key results, you can use the final key result class, which is called the balancing or paired key result.

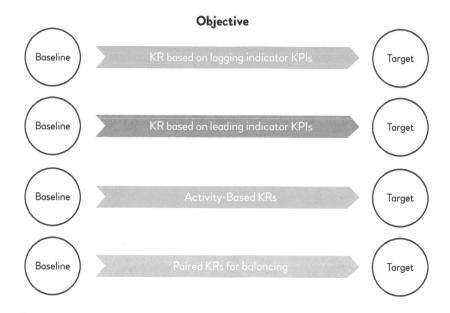

Figure 3.11: *A representation of all the classes of key results you can use within your organization to create strong, effective OKRs.*

When companies do use this class of key result, it's usually to address quality or efficiency. All teams need to strike a careful balance between speed and quality, producing as fast as possible without sacrificing the quality of what they are producing.

These key results are used to ensure that people don't lose sight of the importance of quality, which is entirely possible when team members are focusing on KPIs and tangible outcomes.

Do all OKRs have to have this kind of a structure?

Not all OKRs follow the structure laid out above. Different levels of the company require different classess of key results in order to measure progress and fulfill objectives. Usually, though, the distribution of these key result classes varies as shown in figure 3.12.

The distribution of these four classes of key results will necessarily vary across the three most common levels of OKRs: the corporate, department, and team levels.

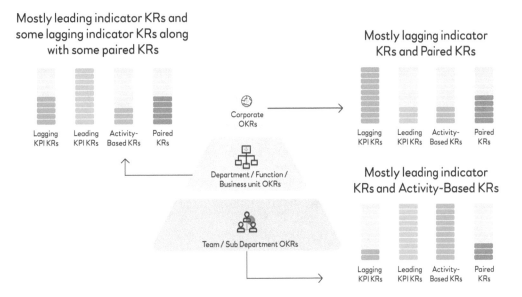

Figure 3.12: *This image shows how each OKR level uses the four classes of key results.*

At the corporate OKR level, you will see mostly lagging indicators. Additionally, there are sometimes a few paired OKRs to help break up any KPI-exclusive tunnel vision your team might have. This isn't to say that a corporate level never uses leading indicators to create key results, however that class of key result should be used sparingly at this level of an organization.

For example, take a look at the OKR to Grow Our Revenue in figure 3.13. Three of the four key result classes are represented in the five key results.

KR1: Increase ARR from $3M to $10M

KR2: Increase Implementation Revenue from $0M to $7M

KR3: Increase Expansion revenue from $0M to $2M

Key results one, two, and three are all lagging indicators. These targets directly measure the success of the objective because they are tracking revenue.

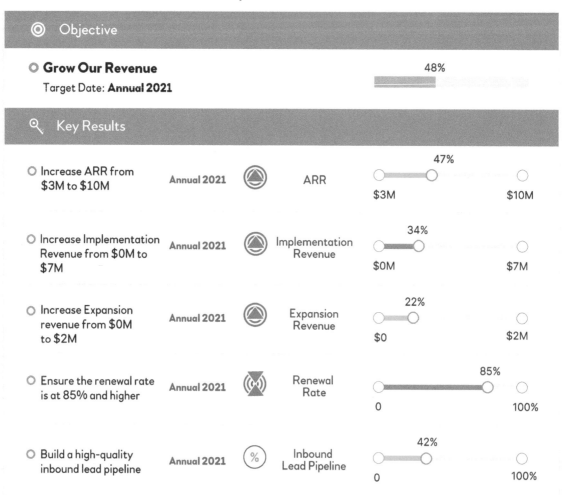

Figure 3.13: An OKR to "Grow Our Revenue" with all classes of key result to help measure the success of the goal.

KR4: Ensure the renewal rate is at 85% and higher

Meanwhile, the fourth key result to maintain the renewal rate at 85% or higher is a balanced key result that will help the business maintain the quality of their service.

KR 5: Build a high-quality inbound lead pipeline

The fifth key result can be considered an activity-based key result– and in the next example, this will be cascaded down as an objective for the marketing department.

At the middle level of an organization in the department or business unit level, you will start to see more leading indicators. Lagging indicators, and perhaps a few balanced or paired key results will be mixed in with these leading indicators, but the majority will always be leading indicator-based key results. This is because department OKRs are commonly aligned with the

Marketing Department OKR

◎ Objective				
Build a High-Quality Inbound Lead Pipeline Target Date: **Q3 - 2021**				38%

🔍 Key Results				
○ Generate at least 1000 leads per week through our website	Q3 - 2021		Leads	8% — 0 to 1000
○ Ensure at least 50% of the leads generated through the website are high-quality	Q3 - 2021		Lead quality	50% — 0 to 100%
○ Produce and rollout amazing content	Q3 - 2021	%	Content Rollout	30% — 0 to 100%
○ Increase # of new users visiting website each week from 30k to 50k	Q3 - 2021		New Users	39k — 30k to 50k
○ Increase CTR of Google Ads from 2% to 5%	Q3 - 2021		CTR	3% — 2% to 5%

company level OKRs, and they will use KPIs that help the corporate level achieve their goals.

Let's take a look at an OKR for the marketing department:

KR 1: Generate at least 1000 leads per week through our website

The first key result for this marketing department OKR is a lagging indicator. This is a lagging indicator because the success of this target informs us about the quality of the lead pipeline. Our target here is directly measuring the objective.

However, if this key result were to appear at the company level, for example, it would be a leading indicator. This is because leads directly affect the ability to generate revenue. If a business does not generate enough leads, it won't be possible to reach its revenue goal. Yet, even if they do reach their lead target, it's far from a sure thing— there are still more components in the sales process that come before revenue. Generating quality leads each week is just one part of hitting your target successfully.

KR 2: Ensure at least 50% of the leads generated through the website are high-quality

The second key result to ensure that 50% of the leads generated through the site are high-quality is a balanced key result, which is important to have at this level, though not very common.

KR 3: Produce and rollout amazing content

The third key result, to produce and roll out content, is an activity-based key result. This key result can be completed through posting blog posts, tutorial videos, and adding support content to attract new customers and help them learn about the company's product. This key result can be assigned as an objective to a sub-department or team for them to expand on and create key results that can specifically track this target.

KR 4: Increase # of new users visiting website each week from 30k to 50k

KR 5: Increase CTR of Google Ads from 2% to 5%

Lastly, key results four and five are both leading indicators, since these KPIs will impact the production of leads, but do not directly measure leads themselves.

Finally, at the operational level, you might have a few lagging indicator key results and some balanced key results, but mostly you will see leading indicator key results and activity-based key results.

Let's take a look at the content team's OKR at the functional level (Fig. 3.14).

This OKR demonstrates the standard distribution of key results at the sub-department, team, or individual level of a company.

KR 1: Generate at least 25k new website visitors per week

The first key result to generate at least 25k new website visitors per week, is a leading indicator for this content OKR. Leading indicators are common at the operational level.

KR 2: Generate 100k page views per week from new visitors

The second key result is a lagging indicator. The number of page views not only corresponds to our leading indicator about the number of new website visitors, but also is directly affected by the quality of the e-books, blogs, and infographics rolled out, which should all drive traffic to the site. Lagging indicator key results aren't common at this level of the organization, but are still an effective way to measure progress.

KR 3: Publish 6 e-books on strategies to manage your business

KR 4: Publish 40 blogs targeted at HR professionals to improve employee engagement and performance

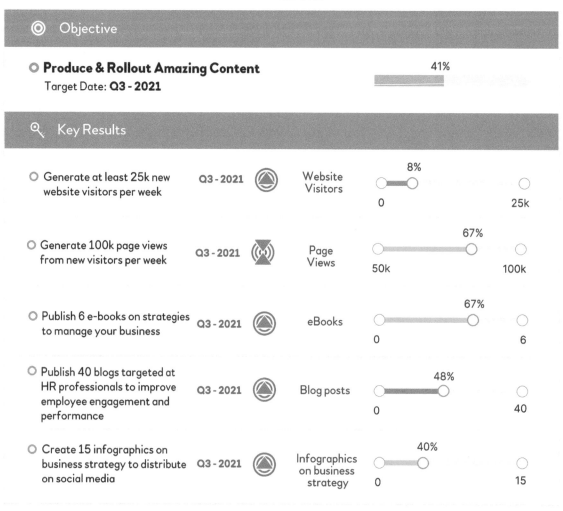

Content Team OKR

Figure 3.14: A strong example of an OKR at the team level. This OKR is for the Content Team.

KR 5: Create 15 infographics on business strategy to distribute on social media

Key results three, four, and five are all activity-based key results. These key results are usually measured using tasks.

Activity-based key results are common at this level of an organization. These measure important tasks or processes that impact the success of the objective, which in turn impacts the aligned OKRs on the department and company levels.

Final Thoughts

As you and your team write OKRs for your company, you'll want to keep in mind the bigger picture of your organization. KPIs used at the company level most likely won't work for key results at the department or individual level. Keeping a close eye on what kind of key results your team is writing, and how each tier of the company feeds into one another, is all part of having a strong OKR program.

Like any skill, writing great key results will become easier with time. As a leader, you can make a point to maintain full transparency in your organization, as well as ensure your team has the required tools to write and execute their OKRs.

How do you write good OKRs?

4

What is Alignment?

Focus **Alignment** **Commitment** **Tracking** **Stretching**

Alignment is one of the core principles of OKRs. The first step for an enterprise-wide OKR implementation is to set the company-level or department-level OKRs, depending on the OKR levels you have rolled out in your organization.

Large enterprises may start with OKR implementations at the department level, rolling out OKRs for their engineering, marketing, strategy, and customer success departments. Start-ups to medium size companies may choose to begin their implementations at the company level.

If a company decides to do enterprise-wide implementation, typically the CEO/Chief of Staff/President defines the OKRs at the company level.

For example, let us say an upcoming tech start-up has an objective defined as "Become a highly desired employer." This objective may have to be achieved by the contribution of multiple teams. HR needs to roll out policies and compensation plans, coupled with a great environment that makes the company desirable for knowledgeable workers.

Marketing can promote interesting projects that the design and engineering department undertake in order to bolster their brand marketing and communicate the desired message to the target audience. The engineering department can create a rigorous work environment that encourages outstanding work. This helps bring out the best in team members, motivate employees to stay with the company, and helps the company create trend-setting products.

In this case, for the company-level Objective of "Become a highly desired employer," the HR, Engineering, and Marketing departments may have to create OKRs and align with the company OKR. This would be a form of top-down alignment, as the company's key results are informing the priorities for each department.

If a company is doing a department-level implementation (for example, Marketing), then the OKRs are first defined at the department level.

Marketing may have five sub-departments: email marketing, inbound marketing, social media, traditional channels, and SEO. The CMO or VP of Marketing defines OKRs first and "assigns" relevant OKRs to each of the 5 sub-departments. This method of cascading OKRs can also be referred to as top-down alignment or assignment.

Alternatively, each of the five sub-departments can first create their OKRs and align them upwards to inform the marketing department's OKRs. In this scenario, employees are empowered to identify their sub-department's top priorities and goals for a quarter, and connect those to the larger organization, enabling them to directly impact the trajectory and success of the business itself. Let's focus on two simple ways to accomplish cascading OKRs, or top-down alignment, and how to initiate rolling up OKRs, or bottom-up alignments.

Cascading OKRs

You can align your OKRs by assigning your key result as an objective or a key result to departments, teams, or individuals. This way, the assignee will receive that objective or key result as a priority.

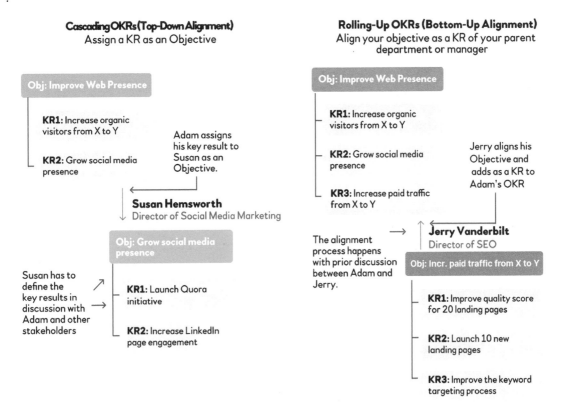

Figure 4.1: This image demonstrates how OKRs are cascaded or rolled up between companies, departments, and teams.

Consider the following OKR example to Improve Web Presence. Adam, the VP of Marketing, is working on this OKR. If he needs assistance, he can assign his key results to other employees as objectives or as key results.

Adam Holmes
VP of Marketing

Obj: Improve Web Presence

KR1: Increase organic visitors from X to Y

KR2: Grow social media presence

Assigning a key result as an objective:

If Adam were to assign his key result as an objective, the assignee would then write their own key results to help accomplish their assignment. The assignee will need to figure out how to write and complete their key results.

If Adam assigns the Key Result to Susan as an Objective, then Susan must define key results by discussing strategies and outcomes with Adam and other stakeholders. Because Adam's key result is aligned from the top-down to Susan's OKR, any progress she makes will help move the needle on Adam's key result, and his OKR as a whole.

Assigning a key result as a key result:

If Adam assigns his key result as a key result, the outcome that must be fulfilled is clear. Adam might assign this key result to someone else because he does not have the bandwidth to complete it himself.

In this scenario illustrated in figure 4.2, Adam adds his key result to another existing objective or a newly created one. In our example, Adam delegates his key result to Jerry, who adds it to a relevant objective he already had in his priorities for the quarter. Any progress Jerry makes will contribute to both Jerry's separate OKR, as well as Adam's original OKR.

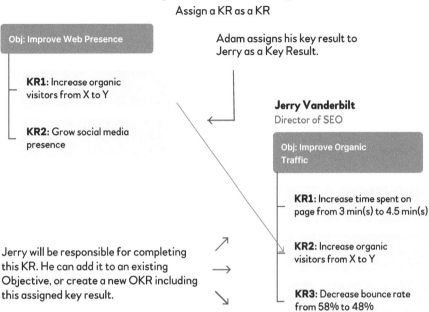

Cascading OKRs (Top-Down Alignment)
Assign a KR as a KR

Obj: Improve Web Presence

KR1: Increase organic visitors from X to Y

KR2: Grow social media presence

Adam assigns his key result to Jerry as a Key Result.

Jerry Vanderbilt
Director of SEO

Obj: Improve Organic Traffic

KR1: Increase time spent on page from 3 min(s) to 4.5 min(s)

Jerry will be responsible for completing this KR. He can add it to an existing Objective, or create a new OKR including this assigned key result.

KR2: Increase organic visitors from X to Y

KR3: Decrease bounce rate from 58% to 48%

Figure 4.2: *This image demonstrates how upper-level leaders can cascade important key results downward as key results for others.*

Rolling Up OKRs

In contrast to cascading OKRs, there may be instances where alignments must come from the bottom-up and Objectives must be rolled up to the next level. There are times where individual contributors may have more insight into customers' thoughts or other ideas that do not necessarily reach the executive level. Including employees' ideas and contributions in an OKR adds an extra incentive for them to invest in its success.

For example, if Jerry has an objective that contributes to Adam's objective to improve web presence, he could opt to roll up his objective to "Increase paid traffic from X to Y" as a key result to Adam's objective. Any progress that Jerry makes on the key results for his objective will impact the progress of his OKR, as well as the progress of Adam's OKR, since the two are aligned.

Connections like this should be discussed prior to alignment to ensure that it is the best choice for the goals both Adam and Jerry want to achieve.

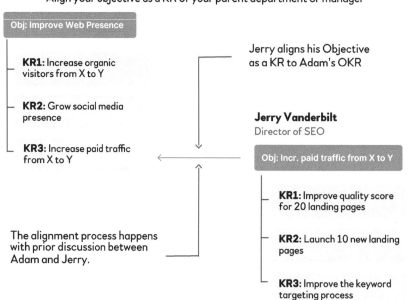

Rolling-Up OKRs (Bottom-Up Alignment)

Align your objective as a KR of your parent department or manager

Obj: Improve Web Presence

KR1: Increase organic visitors from X to Y

KR2: Grow social media presence

KR3: Increase paid traffic from X to Y

Jerry aligns his Objective as a KR to Adam's OKR

Jerry Vanderbilt
Director of SEO

Obj: Incr. paid traffic from X to Y

KR1: Improve quality score for 20 landing pages

KR2: Launch 10 new landing pages

KR3: Improve the keyword targeting process

The alignment process happens with prior discussion between Adam and Jerry.

Figure 4.3: This demonstrates how rolling up OKRs works. Objectives flow from the bottom-up to align as key results on higher-level OKRs.

5

How do you balance cascading and rolling up OKRs?

Consistent alignment of capabilities and internal processes with the customer value proposition is the core of any strategy execution.

 **Robert S. Kaplan**

As discussed earlier in this book, alignment is one of the critical pillars of the OKR philosophy.

Organizations achieve alignment using a top-down and a bottom-up approach— also known as cascading or rolling up. Some organizations want to commit to just one alignment approach, but it rarely works, and can make an OKR program unnecessarily rigid. You can certainly start with one approach and then begin using other approaches as needed. This is a practical alternative to simply commiting to one method. So, let's be clear at the outset; the extent of cascading and rolling up OKRs will be different at different levels of the organization.

Middle management plays a crucial role in striking a balance between cascading and rolling up OKRs.

As a middle manager you are in effect a chief executive of an organization yourself... as a micro CEO, you can improve performance and productivity, whether or not the rest of the company follows suit.

Andy Grove
Former CEO of Intel

A lot has been written about the importance of middle management. A 2011 study conducted by Wharton professor Ethan Mollick summarizes that: "Top management plays a significant role in setting the company's overall direction, but they don't have a big part in deciding which individual projects are selected and how they are run. It's all about the middle managers."

Alignment

When it comes to alignment, middle management plays a crucial role in execution, as well as translating what top management wants for the lower-level employees.

Focus　　　**Alignment**　　　**Commitment**　　　**Tracking**　　　**Stretching**

As you can imagine, the upper layers of an organization usually roll OKRs from the bottom-up, while the lower tiers of a company have goals cascaded to them from the top-down. Let's take a five-level example of the C-Suite, VPs, directors, managers, and team members. You may have VPs reporting to multiple levels of directors and managers, but this is a simple representation of alignment:

Level	Alignment	
	Top-Down	Bottom-Up
C Suite	▽	
VPs	▽	▲
Directors	▼	△
Managers	▼	△
Team Members		△

▼ ▲ – Most Likely   ▽ △ – Somewhat Likely

Figure 5.1: This graph demonstrates how cascading down and rolling-up OKRs commonly works within an organization.

In an organization, the top management sets the corporate objectives, which are informed by the company's vision and strategy. The C-Suite relies heavily on the VPs to align upwards to the objectives that they set at the company level. Under the guidance of these overarching company goals, departments can create OKRs that address both the priorities of certain departments, as well as the goals of the company. VPs can align departmental objectives up to the company level as key results for the corporate objectives.

In theory, this happens in three steps:

- The C-Suite establishes annual or quarterly objectives.

- VPs understand the objectives and prepare what their objectives (and possibly key results) should be.

- The VPs' objectives are rolled up and set up as the key results for the C-Suite.

In practice, this happens collectively across many objectives of the C-Suite and can be a very complicated process. But with practice, the quality of this exercise will be very revealing and set the tone for the quarter of the entire organization.

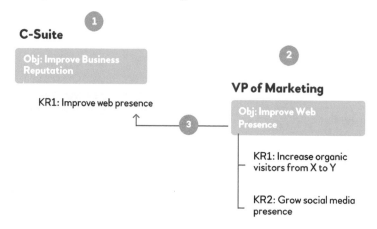

Figure 5.2: *This figure gives an example of how a VP can roll their objective from the bottom-up as a key result for the C-Suite.*

Objectives

Depending on the company, the executive team might choose to come up with the objectives for the entire business's key functions, or allow VPs to create their own OKRs and align upwards. As with most things in the OKR framework, the details depend on the organization in question. Typically, companies will usually have a mix of delegated objectives and original objectives.

You might find that if a certain department function is critical to the success of a company's

Level	Objectives	
	Initiated by themselves	Delegated from higher levels
C-Suite	●	
VPs	●	○
Directors	○	●
Managers	○	●
Team Members		●

● – Most Likely   ○ – Somewhat Likely

Figure 5.3: A chart depicting how likely an OKR level within an organization is to initiate OKRs by themselves or have OKRs delegated from a higher level

objective, VPs will be assigned a key result as their objective from the corporate level. Meanwhile, if a function is not vital to a company's objective, VPs will have the freedom to come up with their own objectives and align them upwards.

Whether or not a function is vital to a company's objectives is not permanent. A function that is vital in one quarter may not be in the next quarter. Bottlenecks might arise, and managers need to be aware of this and ready to help resolve roadblocks.

Directors and managers are in a similar boat as VPs. There is a mix of original and delegated objectives. But the extent of the mix will vary depending on circumstances. And when it comes to individual contributors (team members), objectives most certainly get delegated from above. There is very little chance for individual team members to create their own objectives.

Key results

As previously discussed, the C-Suite focuses on setting goals that adhere to the company's long-term strategy. These high-level objectives guide the rest of the business in creating and executing their objectives.

For the most part, the key results for company-level objectives are generally created through bottom-up alignment from the next level of the management.

At the department level, it is more likely that VPs, directors, and managers write key results for the sector of the business they are responsible for, though it is still possible that they use key results aligned up from the cross-functional team level. Depending on the sector, the amount of original key results versus the delegated or aligned key results varies. This is what makes being a middle manager challenging.

Level	Key Results		
	Initiated by themselves	Delegated from higher levels	Aligned from lower levels
C-Suite	○		●
VPs	●	○	●
Directors	●	●	○
Managers	●	●	○
Team Members	○	●	

● – Most Likely   ○ – Somewhat Likely

Figure 5.4: *A chart depicting how likely each OKR level is to initiate an OKR by themselves, delegate an OKR from a higher level, or to have an OKR aligned from a lower level.*

A disciplined OKR program can make challenges less daunting and make the job of a middle manager easier to a certain extent. The visibility, transparency, and alignment aspects of the

OKR methodology help middle management get the business moving in the right direction at a much faster pace.

When it comes to individual contributors (team members), key results are usually delegated from managers or heavily informed by higher levels of the organization. Individual team members will almost always see alignment from the top-down rather than the bottom-up.

Final Thoughts

Middle management plays a crucial role in communicating the top-level vision to the teams that execute that vision. This "sandwich layer" is responsible for intelligently striking a balance between cascading and rolling up OKRs to achieve clarity in communicating the company's vision to everyone in the organization. Middle managers ensure that teams are focusing on the right priorities, measuring what impacts the business most, and achieving goals that contribute towards the overall success of the organization— not just specific sectors of it.

How do you balance cascading and rolling up OKRs?

6

Is it necessary to use KPIs in OKRs?

Are OKRs replacing KPIs?

Many teams that are just starting out with the OKR methodology might wonder if OKRs are an alternative to KPIs, or Key Performance Indicators. The answer is no; OKRs do not and cannot replace your company's KPIs. These two acronyms serve different purposes and cannot replace each other.

While OKRs cannot replace KPIs themselves, they can replace several methods of managing your KPIs. KPIs and their trends indicate how well your business is doing, or how parts of your business are doing.

KPIs can be used in order to accurately measure key results. Setting key results to increase, decrease, or maintain KPIs at a certain value is a good way to set targets as well as measure the health of your business and the success of your objectives.

Another way to look at this is to think of OKRs as the process of taking a KPI from value A to value B. Just by this definition, it is evident that OKRs operate on KPIs and are not replacing them in any way.

Figure 6.1: This image shows how OKRs and KPIs relate to one another. OKRs are a way to report on KPIs and review their changes within your business.

A few typical follow-up questions in a conversation about OKRs and KPIs are as follows:

- How are OKRs and KPIs different?

- How are they similar?

- Why do we need OKRs if we have KPIs?

KPI.org defines KPIs as follows– *"Key Performance Indicators (KPIs) are the critical (key) indicators of progress toward an intended result."* KPIs have been wildly popular in the last two to three decades.

At the most basic level, KPIs measure an aspect of a business. Let us look at each term in the phrase and see how they are defined.

- **Key**– provides a means of achieving or understanding something.

- **Performance**– defines a particular action, deed, or proceeding.

- **Indicator**– designates the state or level of something.

You can measure revenue, revenue per employee, revenue per sales rep, and so on. There are literally thousands of such measurements that can indicate how a business is doing. Among those thousands, you select the few that are key indicators for your business and for the appropriate business functions. These are your key performance indicators. Simply put, a KPI serves to perform a health check on the productivity, effectiveness, and efficiency of staff, employees, and teams.

A few KPIs that businesses commonly use are:

- Revenue

- Net Profit Margin

- EBITDA

- Average Time for Conversion

- Net Sales– Dollar or Percentage Growth

- Number of New Contracts Signed Per Period

KPIs and Key Results

A key part of understanding OKRs vs KPIs is understanding how OKRs work in relationship to KPIs, and you can leverage them both. Understanding this relationship is vital to getting the most out of your key metrics as well as your OKR program.

So, when does a KPI become an OKR?

Once you have identified the KPI you want to track, you must first baseline it, and find the

KPI + Base-lined + Target + Time-frame + Owner → **Key Result**

Figure 6.2: This equation shows how a KPI becomes a key result. Rather than replacing KPIs, OKRs instead use them to accurately track important targets.

value that your business, department, or team is currently performing at. Then, based on your baseline value, you'll set a target. For example, if your KPI is Revenue, and you're currently performing at $3M, you'll want to set an ambitious, but not unattainable, target. In this example, you might set the target for $5M.

Then, you must add a timeframe within which you'd like to achieve this target. OKRs are usually set up on a quarterly or annual basis. Finally, assign a department, team, or individual who owns this target and is responsible for tracking progress and completing check-ins for this target.

Once a KPI has all these features, it has become a well-structured key result to add to an objective (Figure 6.2).

OKRs vs KPIs

OKRs may be a relatively new goal-setting framework, but every business has a plan and a budget for every year. These plans and corresponding budgets typically include projections of KPIs based on what you did in the past and what you expect to achieve this year. This is where OKRs come into play.

Let's take a look at a travel analogy to better understand how OKRs and KPIs work together. Imagine you are driving to some place. If your goal is your destination, your OKR is the vehicle, and your KPI is the dashboard. Your OKR is what gets you to the final destination, whereas

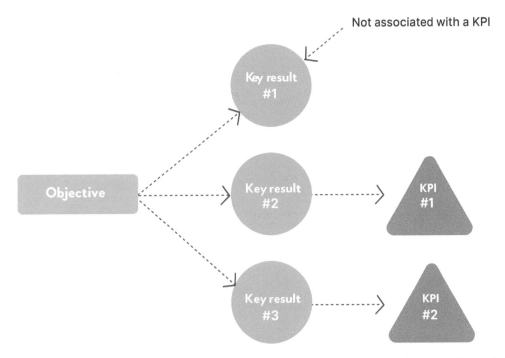

Figure 6.3: This illustration shows how KPIs can be associated with a key result, but that is not always the case.

your KPI tells you how your car is doing as it makes its way toward the goal. One can use OKRs and KPIs to achieve the same objective– but they perform different functions.

OKRs provide a simple and powerful approach to set business targets, measure progress, and achieve greater success. Extending the travel analogy, you can use the dashboard to check on the KPIs such as fuel level, engine oil level, vehicle speed, etc.

But there are other things that you care about that are not in any dashboards. For example, hiring a VP of sales for Europe is not a KPI-based key result, however it's important to the success of the objective to "Grow Revenue" (Figure 6.4). If you ignore this key result and don't commit to seeing it through, your business will be worse off– so ensure that you are paying attention to both measurable and non-measurable key results throughout the quarter.

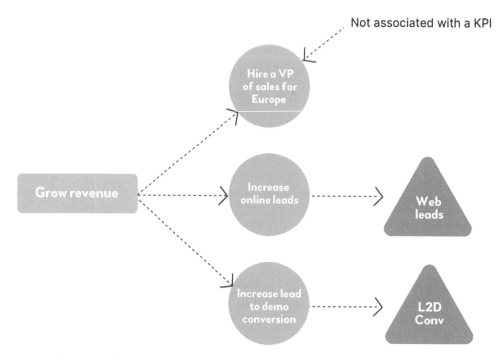

Figure 6.4: Examples of key results that are KPI-based and a key result that is not.

Move from Percentage-Tracked to KPI-based key results

When getting started with OKRs, the biggest challenge you face is how to define a good OKR. Defining an objective ("What do you want to achieve?") may not seem difficult as compared to setting key results ("How are you going to achieve this?") to many users.

For example, delivering fantastic customer support is the top priority for the customer support team. This is their objective. Meanwhile, key results are derived by asking the following question: "What outcomes do I need to see in my organization to ensure that we are delivering fantastic customer support?"

Generally, there are seven different types of key results that users can set based on their maturity level with the OKR framework, as well as the nature of the key result they would like to measure (Figure 6.5). The options are:

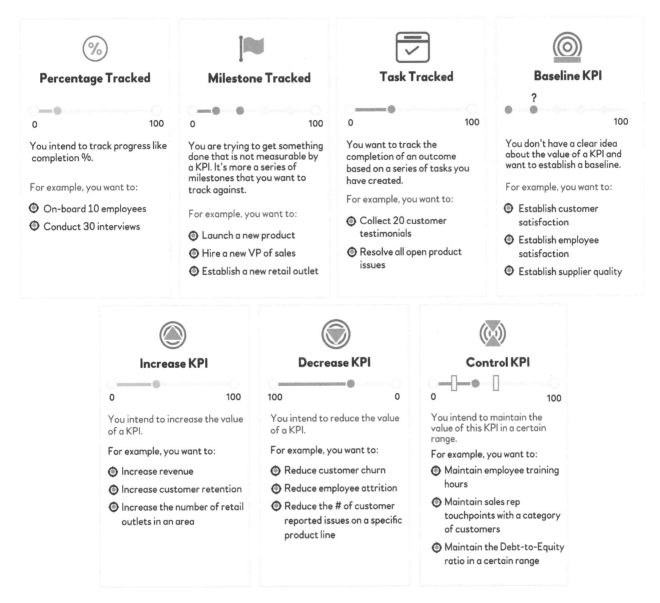

Figure 6.5: The seven common types of key results.

- Percentage-Tracked Key Result

- Milestone-Tracked Key Result

- Task-Tracked Key Result

- Baseline KPI Key Result

- Increase KPI Key Result

- Decrease KPI Key Result

- Control KPI Key Result

Defining effective key results is vital for the success of your OKR implementation, since key results measure the achievement of the objective they are associated with.

Many users new to the OKR framework begin with using the percentage-tracked key result type. This is the simplest way to track key result progress, but it also relies on subjective input from the user and is less concrete than using a KPI-based key result type, which gives objective evidence of progress— or lack thereof.

Percentage-Tracked as KPI-based

For example, say you had a key result to double the amount of employee wellbeing activities this quarter. This key result can be tracked using the percentage-tracked key result type. In order to measure this key result more accurately, you could instead track this as a KPI-based key result (Figure 6.6).

You can use "employee wellbeing activities" as a KPI for this marketing key result. Your key result would then be: "Organize at least 6 employee wellbeing activities".

This switch is beneficial because there is no need to estimate the percentage of the key result

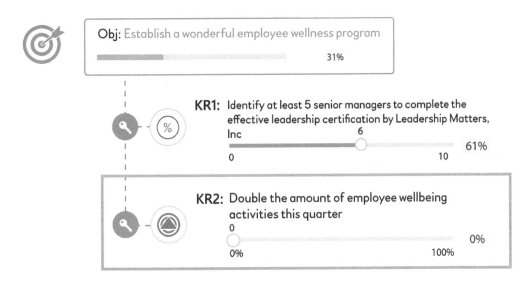

Figure 6.6: The highlighted key result is not based on a KPI, however, it could be with some adjustments.

you have completed each check-in— instead, you can simply measure the number of employee wellbeing activities directly (Figure 6.7).

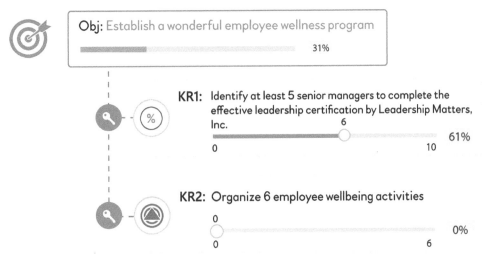

Figure 6.7: The second key result is now tracked using a KPI, making this a stronger key result.

Is it necessary to use KPIs in OKRs?

7

Which type of key result is best?

When you are brand new to OKRs, it seems like there is a lot to learn. You probably have a lot of questions that need to be clarified. While it's true there's a learning curve when it comes to mastering OKRs, it's important that you and your team press forward and get acclimated to this methodology. Eventually, you'll wonder how you ever lived without the framework.

Right now, you're probably still trying to grasp the specific details of OKRs. In this chapter, we're going to take a closer look at key results and key result creation.

One of the most confusing parts of OKRs for new users is how to properly set your key results.

You can boil down key results into seven distinct types, as we discussed in the previous chapter. But how do you know which key result type to choose in any given situation? The decision flow documented below (Figure 7.1) is a simple guide to help you make that choice.

Key Result Types

Let's go through this process in a step-by-step fashion, starting off with a very telling question:

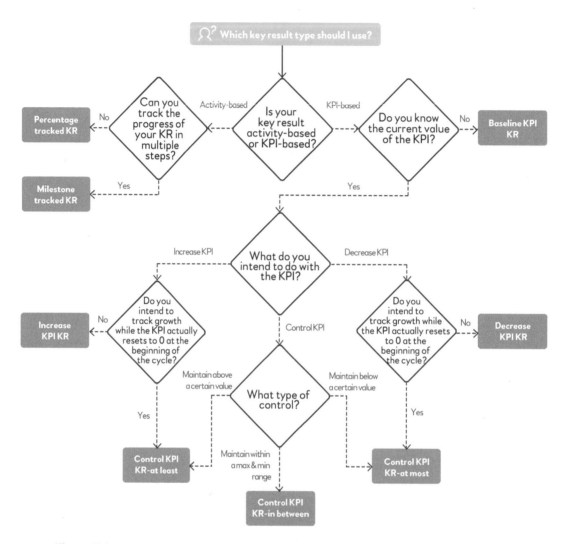

Figure 7.1: *A question & answer flowchart to help OKR users determine which of the seven key result types they should use.*

Is your key result KPI-based or activity-based?

Examples of **KPIs** are:

- Revenue

- New customers

- Customer complaints

- Employee satisfaction scores

Examples of **activities** are:

- Hiring a Sales manager

- Developing a Sales plan

Depending on the topic or focus of your key result, you'll choose one of these options.

For this example, we'll select *activity-based*, since it's a more straightforward way to evaluate progress on paper. The next question then becomes: **Can you track the progress of your activity-based key result in multiple steps or milestones?**

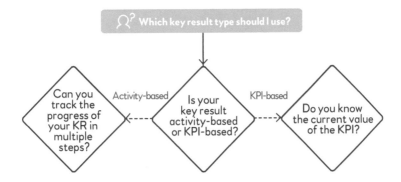

For example, a key result like **"hire a Sales manager"** can have multiple steps, such as:

- Advertise the open position

- Screen and select top 10 candidates

- Phone screen the 10 candidates

- Select top 3 for an in-person interview

- Select the top candidate

- Make an offer

- Launch the onboarding process

Activity-Based Key Results

Can you track this key result using milestones?

If you can track the progress of your key result in multiple steps, or milestones, you can use the milestone-tracked key result type.

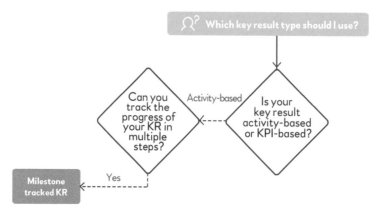

Can you track this key result using percent progress?

Let us take another example, "Prepare product launch budget." While you can drill down and come up with specific steps to track, this activity-based key result might be a less predictable process than is required to set clear milestones. Instead, you may be better off indicating the status in terms of percentage completed.

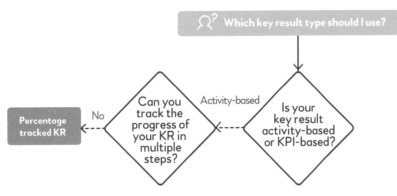

And in this case, we'll take the "percentage tracked" key result path.

Can you track this key result using tasks?

If you have a key result that can be measured with the completion of certain tasks, you can create a "task-tracked" key result type. For example, if you have a key result to publish 30 user tutorial videos, you can track the creation and publication of these videos in a task board, and link them to your key result. Each time you mark a task as "done," your key result progress will increase.

KPI-Based Key Results

Now, let's switch gears and look down the KPI-Based key result type path. This means that we have a tangible metric in mind that we are trying to improve, also known as a KPI.

Do you know the current (baseline) value of the KPI?

Begin by finding your starting value, also known as your baseline value. This is the value you are looking to improve upon for the good of your organization, and the success of your objective. If you don't know the KPI's current value, you should first have a key result to determine the value. This key result type is called a "Baseline KPI". With this key result type, you will define steps you must take in order to find out your baseline metric.

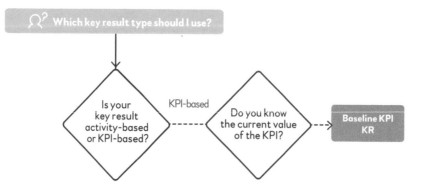

What do you intend to do with the KPI?

If you know the baseline value of the KPI you are working with, you can elect to set a target in three ways; i.e., use one of three different key result types: Control KPI, Increase KPI, or Decrease KPI.

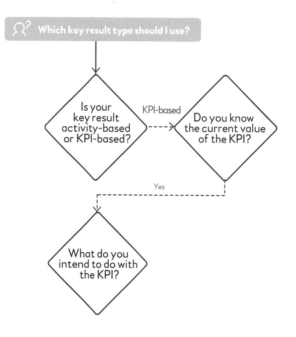

Let's take the Control KPI path first.

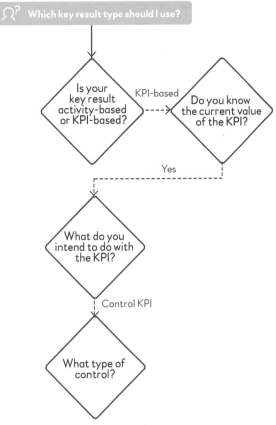

Ways to Measure Control KPI Key Results

Control KPIs are used when you want to keep the value of a KPI in between a range of a minimum and a maximum value.

For example, you may want to maintain the training time that employees attend in a given week within 1-3 hours. In that case, you should set a key result with the KPI "employee training hours" and maintain that value between one and three hours every week. Each time you check-in, you want to ensure that employees have spent at least one hour training, but no more than three hours.

You can also set Control KPIs to keep a value above a minimum threshold; for example, when you want to release at least four articles per week to your blog.

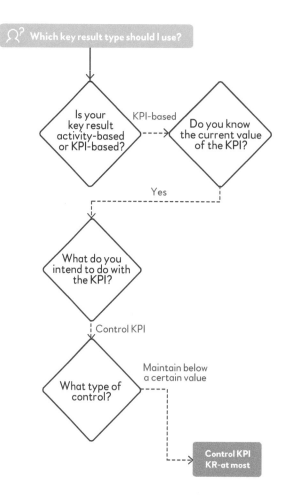

Finally, you can also set Control KPIs to keep a value below a certain maximum. So, if you would like your Customer Success to answer all customer emails within 24 hours, you can set your key result using a control KPI and write "Maintain the average email response time under 24 hours".

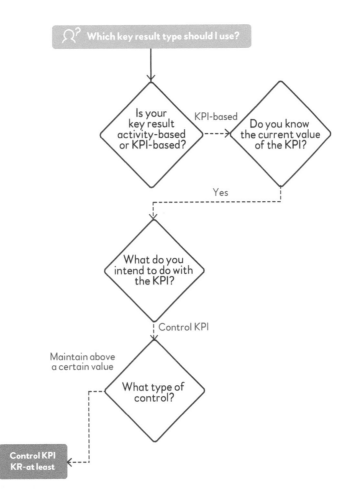

Increase KPI

Let's say you would like to increase your KPI. With certain KPIs, the higher the value, the better. For example: Revenue, CSAT Score, Employee Satisfaction Score, and so on.

Are you tracking incremental increase, while the KPI starts from zero in the new cycle?

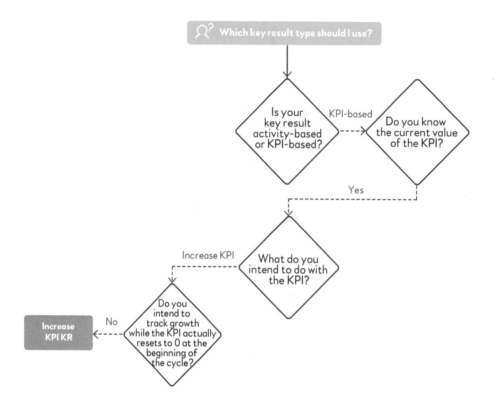

If the answer is "no," then your starting value is not 0– instead, it is your current value. For example, you might have a key result to increase the net promoter score from 60 to 70. When you go from one cycle to another, you start from where you left off. In that case, it's straightforward: choose Increase KPI.

Alternatively, you may want to increase a KPI such as revenue from $3M to $6M in the new cycle.

If we model this as an "Increase KPI" key result, you'll have problems checking in for a few weeks because you need to build up the revenue to $3M to enter the measurement spectrum.

In this case, it is better to just model the key result to go from $0 to $6M.

Decrease KPI

Let's say you would like to decrease a KPI such as Customer Churn, Defect Score, Employee Attrition, and so on.

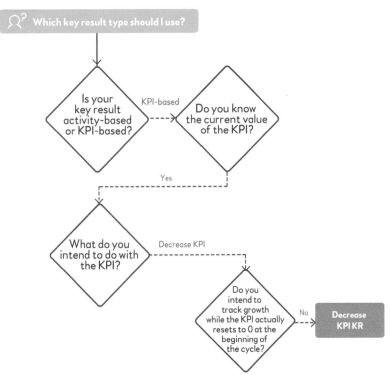

When tracking KPIs you would like to decrease, you do not start with a value of zero. When you transition from one quarter to the next, you build on progress as well– so the progress you make by reducing the customer churn in Q1 can carry over into Q2, and you can set an even more ambitious target than in the last quarter.

Which type of key result is best?

8

How do you check-in? What is a good time frame for check-ins?

No matter how large or small a project is, managers need a reliable method for making sure their teams are in sync. This will help ensure alignment, stay on schedule, maintain forward momentum, and maximize productivity.

What is PPP?

The Progress, Plans, and Problems (PPP) framework is an effective method used by many successful brands with a higher OKR maturity— including Apple, Facebook, and Skype.

This powerful, yet simple framework guides teams or individuals to think about:

Progress

Plans

Problems

- **Progress**– What has been achieved in the last period?

- **Plans**– What will be completed in the next period?

- **Problems**– What are the foreseen challenges or roadblocks for each employee or the team?

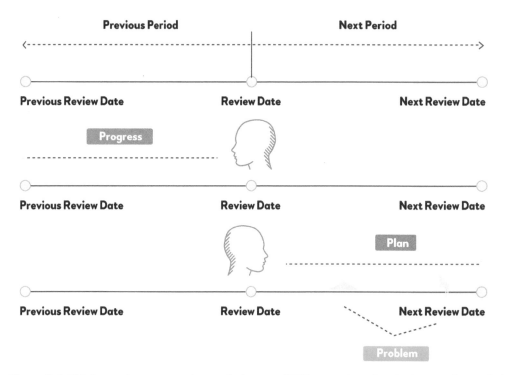

Figure 8.1: This image demonstrates how each element of PPP comes into play during a review period.

Using the PPP Framework, managers can stay on top of their team's short- and long-term OKRs without disrupting productivity, thereby eliminating the need for excessive meetings, or creating undue employee stress by not setting clear expectations.

PPP is an ideal status reporting method for goal-oriented companies. It keeps all team members focused on their individual OKRs instead of becoming overwhelmed by the enormity of the big picture.

PPP on OKRs keeps the entire team on the same page. It can also help individual team members set better personal targets, remain on task, and plan realistic goals.

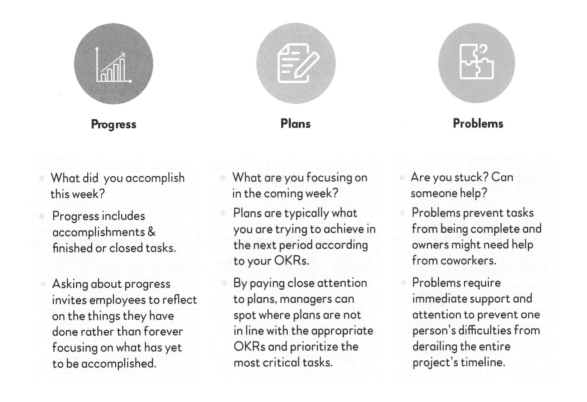

Progress

- What did you accomplish this week?
- Progress includes accomplishments & finished or closed tasks.
- Asking about progress invites employees to reflect on the things they have done rather than forever focusing on what has yet to be accomplished.

Plans

- What are you focusing on in the coming week?
- Plans are typically what you are trying to achieve in the next period according to your OKRs.
- By paying close attention to plans, managers can spot where plans are not in line with the appropriate OKRs and prioritize the most critical tasks.

Problems

- Are you stuck? Can someone help?
- Problems prevent tasks from being complete and owners might need help from coworkers.
- Problems require immediate support and attention to prevent one person's difficulties from derailing the entire project's timeline.

During your check-ins— weekly being the most common— all team members receive a reporting reminder from their manager. Then, they submit three items for each PPP category.

Collecting and analyzing these responses allows a manager to offer praise and encouragement where it is due, as well as guide a project's trajectory. Most importantly, it will enable you to address problems before they become challenging to manage.

So, why three?

Three is the most winning number in communications.

The Rule of 3 is everywhere: writing, economics, business, psychology, mathematics, computer programming, religion, and science.

Here are just a few examples:

- Real Estate: "Location, Location, Location"

- Success: "Blood, sweat, and tears"

- Speeches: "Friends, Romans, Countrymen"

- Government: "Of the people, by the people, for the people"

Science suggests that people absorb and remember three groups because three is the lowest number required for pattern recognition, and people love patterns. Keeping to the Rule of 3 also makes sure active working memory is never overloaded— resulting in better retention, and long-term recollection.

Project Status Reports are meant to be short, succinct, and informal. In a busy world, long paragraphs of text are often skimmed or ignored. As an example, look at the popularity of Twitter, where people devour and digest information in bite-sized chunks. Everyone has time to read 140 characters or less.

Applying the same concept to status updates and progress reports keeps employees engaged, while simultaneously providing them with the important information they need to know.

How Does PPP Improve Effectiveness?

By putting everything in writing, teams can avoid unnecessary miscommunication and can

Progress

- Created four landing pages covering the features released on 13-Oct.
- Implemented on-page SEO fixes on 27 landing pages
- Published four new blog posts across three categories

Plan

- Introduce a new blog category to focus on employee engagement
- Promote this category in social media
- Hire a social media analyst

Problem

- Need articles for the new category
- Need HR to find better quality candidates

Figure 8.2: *An example PPP report.*

create a structured log of progress in their organization that spans multiple quarters. A manager can reference the PPP documents, allowing them to judge progress, offer help to anyone struggling, and assign tasks effectively.

Not only does PPP provide a brief, informative way for teams to maintain a log of progress, but there are a number of other benefits to this methodology you should consider:

1. PPP is Cost-Effective

Instead of losing productivity due to potentially lengthy or irrelevant meetings, PPP reports allow managers to keep a finger on their project's pulse without disrupting the team's productivity.

2. PPP is Fast

The PPP template takes minutes to fill out and moments to send. The return on investment

(ROI) of creating a PPP report relative to the time needed for task completion is enormous.

3. PPP is Simple

Every status update involves answering the same three questions. These reports are informal, brief, and specific.

4. PPP Improves Accountability

When goals and tasks are transparent for everyone to see, team members are more likely to follow through with them. When employees know that others can see their progress, and dependent key results are relying on their work, their motivation increases.

5. PPP Connects the Manager to the Team (and the Team to the Manager)

Instead of ineffective or inefficient meetings held at irregular intervals, PPP meetings are held at regular intervals to keep the lines of communication open and expectations clear.

6. PPP Improves Transparency

With the PPP methodology, team members regularly report on their activities, and managers respond to those reports. This enables managers to help resolve employee issues before they can spin out of control, and keeps everyone on the team aware of what everyone else is working on. Ideally, a manager should submit their own PPP report to the team, so the transparency works both ways.

7. PPP Improves Commitment

Because PPP reports require employees to write actionable steps that they will be taking to move forward with their work, team members are less likely to become overwhelmed. Once the manager approves the plans for the week, employees have tangible action items that they can go ahead and execute, ensuring that they will make progress on their important key results.

5 Tips for Implementing PPP

1. Maintain Simplicity

Keep it short. Stick to the **Rule of Three**, and only record progress, plans, and problems.

2. Be Consistent

Keep meetings regular and mandatory. Consistency is the key to forming habits.

3. Foster Collaboration

Some people might struggle with the idea of highlighting their problems. It is too easy to see problems as a personal failure. Promote the idea that discussing issues fosters important collaboration and team building.

4. Communicate Clearly

Keep it in writing. Having written material to refer to provides a long-lasting reference. Before meetings, ensure everyone has read the entire team's progress reports to avoid wasting time on repeating information.

5. Follow Up

Every submitted report is an opportunity to start a conversation. Rather than focusing on what has not been done, offer help, constructive criticism, or encouragement.

Final Thoughts

The Progress, Plans, and Problems (PPP) framework is a tried and true project management technique that is both simple and powerful. This simple framework can help teams provide straightforward, informative, and consistent status updates to all stakeholders within a company.

9

How do you grade your OKRs?

OKR grading is a step or a precursor towards your end of quarter reflection, which is an essential part of any OKR program looking to build on its progress and maximize growth. This is how you can measure the progress you made towards your goal and share successes or learnings with the rest of your team in terms the entire company understands.

Grading OKRs establishes a common platform to evaluate how OKRs are being practiced among different employees, departments, and teams.

If the department heads from Engineering, Marketing, and Sales were to meet in a room at the end of a quarter without OKRs to compare their progress, there would not be any common ground to compare. However, with OKRs and OKR grading, progress is translated into a common language that everyone can understand.

OKR grading measures the success of OKRs in numerical terms. Sales might be able to say that their OKR to *grow revenue* was completed at 0.9, or 90%. Meanwhile, Engineering can share that their OKR to increase product stability was completed at 0.6, or 60%.

How do you grade OKRs?

There are a couple of approaches to grading OKRs:

- Standard Achievement Percentage– Based on a percentage of achievement.

- Custom Key Result Scoring– Bucketed into areas of achievement.

Let us look at this example OKR, "Enhance our customer service." In this case, there are three key results.

Figure 9.1: An OKR for customer service enhancement and its varying progress measurements. For this key result, the customer success team will work closely with the product team.

A simple way to grade OKRs is to grade based on completion percentage. OKR grades are automatically calculated based on the average progress of your key results throughout the quarter.

In general, in the OKR world, the score ranges (Figure 9.2) that are generally accepted are:

- 0 to 30% → Failed to make significant progress.

- 30% to 70% → Progress made but fell short of the finish line.

- 70% to 100% → Delivered as planned.

If you're not interested in using general grades for your OKR program, you could set your own custom values to score your key results and OKR progress and standardize their meaning across your organization.

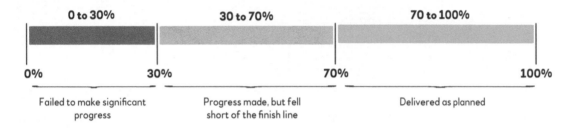

Figure 9.2: *The generally accepted grades and corresponding score ranges for OKRs.*

For instance, you can have four types of base scales to support your scoring:

- 1 → 0 to 1

- 5 → 0 to 5

- 10 → 0 to 10

- 100 → 0 to 100

Now, assuming we take a base scale of one, which many people usually do, you could define your ranges depending on your team's definition of achievement.

You can use three buckets or ranges for your grading scale. This system follows the rule of

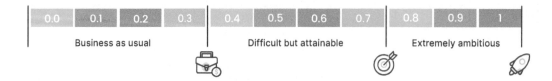

Figure 9.3: *An example of a custom OKR scoring spectrum.*

three we discussed earlier, and is common within the industry.

In this example, we call it:

- Business as usual – when you cross 0.3, or 30%,

- Difficult, but attainable – when you cross 0.7, or 70%

- Extremely Ambitious – when you reach 1.0, or 100%

It is how you would typically categorize your Key Results based on their scores, giving team members another way to view their progress and conceptualize how they performed and achieved within a quarter.

You can modify these ranges however you would like. Extremely ambitious organizations have even modified these ranges like so:

- Business as usual – when you cross 0.7

- Difficult, but attainable – when you cross 0.85

- Extremely ambitious – when you reach 1.0

Which means that until you hit the 0.7 mark, you are not getting to the business as usual level. While this isn't the standard in the OKR framework, it is a choice that leaders can make for their organization.

Final Thoughts

Grading your OKRs gives team members a way to reflect on their performance in the last quarter and think about what initiatives worked, and what ones didn't. Additionally, it helps contextualize progress within your business, so that leaders know what departments and teams need attention and assistance in order to course-correct and improve in the next quarter, or build on existing progress.

10

How do you wrap your OKR quarter?

Strategy-execution frameworks like the OKR framework are an integral part of how businesses are run nowadays. In order to achieve high performance and growth within your company, you must have a system for checking in on each business function and be able to keep your finger on the pulse of company-wide progress.

The OKR methodology requires users to make weekly or biweekly check-ins that help leaders understand the progress that is made throughout the quarter.

We do not learn from experience. We learn from reflecting on experience.

 John Dewey

OKRs, however, are always informed by a bigger picture– such as the long-term strategy of a company, or the mission or vision of the organization. That's why a larger quarterly review is so important for the OKR framework to bring about the most benefits.

The Reflect/Reset process allows your team to review their OKR progress, catalogue what worked, what didn't work, and what changes they can make in future quarters to achieve more. Additionally, it helps everyone smoothly transition into the next quarter, extending or replacing OKRs so that the top priorities are being addressed in each cycle.

The central aspect of Reflect/Reset is this question:

"What are we going to do differently next time?"

This process enables you to 'reflect' on the achievements of the current quarter and apply the learnings to 'reset' them for the next quarter. You can distribute questions for OKR owners to answer to help enhance learning and facilitate a quality reflection process. You then reset the key results for the next quarter.

Insanity: doing the same thing over and over again and expecting different results.

 **Albert Einstein**

The Reflection Process

The reflection process is straightforward. Leaders can define a set of questions that they would like users to answer regarding their OKR progress. These questions can range from general to highly specific. Any information gathered about OKRs will be useful in the coming quarter to help your team achieve more. Some examples of great reflection questions are:

- Did you accomplish your Objective?

- If yes, what contributed to your outcome?

- If not, what challenges did you face?

- What have you learned from the past quarter that might change next quarter's OKR?

- What needs to be adjusted, added, or eliminated from your OKR?

- What did you do in the last quarter that you did not like?

- What do you feel you did well?

- What do you feel you did not do well?

- What do you want to achieve in the next quarter?

These are just sample questions— you can decide what makes sense, and at what levels. Keep in mind that the questions that make sense to ask at the corporate level might not matter at the department level, and vice versa.

The Reset Process

Before you start thinking about resetting your KRs, you should take a look at your Objective.

Is the Objective still relevant for the next quarter? If the answer is yes, then you must examine the Key Results.

At the end of your quarter, your key result progress is either:

- Complete

Or,

- Incomplete

Depending on business conditions, you can either:

- Continue with the Key Result

Or,

- Close the Key Result

Based on these decisions, you can decide the appropriate course of action on each of your key results. When resetting OKRs, you can take a few different actions:

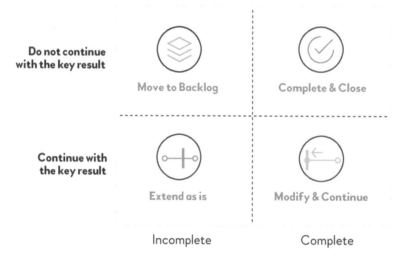

Figure 10.1: This matrix helps you determine what your course of action should be for each of your key results depending on its completion and relevance.

- Complete & Close

- Extend As Is

- Move to Backlog

- Modify & Continue

1. Complete & Close

If you have completed your key result and are satisfied with the value it has reached, you can complete and close the key result to make room for new targets more pertinent to your OKR's success. Make sure to celebrate this accomplishment and record what went right for this OKR.

2. Extend as is

If your key result is incomplete, but still relevant to your OKR's success, you can extend the target as is. For example, if you wanted to establish a retail location in Manhattan, but the project is only 40% complete, your key result is still relevant and should be extended to the next quarter with the same endpoint.

3. Move to backlog

You can move your key result to a backlog, or a list of key result drafts, if it is incomplete but not relevant to the upcoming quarter. Once this key result is relevant again, you can add it to your OKRs.

4. Modify & Continue

This option is used when your key result is complete or nearly complete, and the target is still relevant for the next quarter. However, you might want to modify your target to build on the progress and momentum of the previous quarter. For example, if your key result was to solve 40 issues in your product, but you only resolved 30 issues, you could move the target to a higher number to keep this goal ambitious.

How do you wrap your OKR quarter?

Conclusion

There is no such thing as "a natural" when it comes to OKRs. Everyone from the CEO to your newest hire will have to commit to improving as they go, and help cultivate a culture of learning. This book had provided the details on best practices for rolling out your OKR program to a company of any size, as well as the best methods for keeping execution, engagement, and learning on top priority throughout the entire quarter.

Ensuring that you reinforce these foundational tools and techniques is the key to successfully launching and sustaining your OKR program. Remember that you should take time throughout the first few quarters to answer employees' questions about writing OKRs, selecting the right KPIs, properly completing their check-ins, and reviewing and grading their OKRs. Share this book with your team and help everyone get a solid understanding of how OKRs should fit into their day-to-day work.

Once you have launched your OKR program and have allowed your team to get the hang of OKRs, it's time for you to begin scaling. For expert advice on the smoothest ways to scale your OKR program and grow your business, look for *Scaling your OKR Program*, the final installment in this series.